W9-AXC-872

The Black Death

Titles in the World History Series

The Age of Augustus
The Age of Feudalism
The Age of Pericles
The American Frontier
The American Revolution
Ancient Greece
The Ancient Near East
Architecture
Aztec Civilization
The Black Death
The Byzantine Empire
Caesar's Conquest of Gaul
The California Gold Rush
The Chinese Cultural
   Revolution
The Conquest of Mexico
The Crusades
The Cuban Revolution
The Early Middle Ages
Egypt of the Pharaohs
Elizabethan England
The End of the Cold War
The French and Indian War
The French Revolution
The Glorious Revolution
The Great Depression

Greek and Roman Theater
Hitler's Reich
The Hundred Years' War
The Inquisition
The Italian Renaissance
The Late Middle Ages
The Lewis and Clark
   Expedition
The Mexican Revolution
The Mexican War of
   Independence
Modern Japan
The Punic Wars
The Reformation
The Relocation of the
   North American Indian
The Roman Empire
The Roman Republic
The Russian Revolution
The Scientific Revolution
The Spread of Islam
Traditional Africa
Traditional Japan
The Travels of Marco Polo
The Wars of the Roses
Women's Suffrage

WORLD HISTORY SERIES ■ ■ ■

The Black Death

by
Phyllis Corzine

Lucent Books, P.O. Box 289011, San Diego, CA 92198-9011

Library of Congress Cataloging-in-Publication Data

Corzine, Phyllis, 1943–
    The Black Death / by Phyllis Corzine.
        p. cm. — (World history series)
    Includes bibliographical references and index.
    Summary: Examines the causes, effects, and legacy of the
epidemic that killed millions of people in Europe during the
fourteenth century.
    ISBN 1-56006-299-1 (alk. paper)
    1. Black death—Europe—History—Juvenile literature. [1.
Black death—History. 2. Plague—History. 3. Diseases—History.] I. Title. II. Series.
RC178.A1C67   1997
614.5'732'094—dc20   96-19441
                                                          CIP
                                                           AC

Copyright 1997 by Lucent Books, Inc., P.O. Box 289011,
San Diego, California 92198-9011

Printed in the U.S.A.

Contents

Foreword

Each year on the first day of school, nearly every history teacher faces the task of explaining why his or her students should study history. One logical answer to this question is that exploring what happened in our past explains how the things we often take for granted—our customs, ideas, and institutions—came to be. As statesman and historian Winston Churchill put it, "Every nation or group of nations has its own tale to tell. Knowledge of the trials and struggles is necessary to all who would comprehend the problems, perils, challenges, and opportunities which confront us today." Thus, a study of history puts modern ideas and institutions in perspective. For example, though the founders of the United States were talented and creative thinkers, they clearly did not invent the concept of democracy. Instead, they adapted some democratic ideas that had originated in ancient Greece and with which the Romans, the British, and others had experimented. An exploration of these cultures, then, reveals their very real connection to us through institutions that continue to shape our daily lives.

Another reason often given for studying history is the idea that lessons exist in the past from which contemporary societies can benefit and learn. This idea, although controversial, has always been an intriguing one for historians. Those that agree that society can benefit from the past often quote philosopher George Santayana's famous statement, "Those who cannot remember the past are condemned to repeat it." Historians who ascribe to Santayana's philosophy believe that, for example, studying the events that led up to the major world wars or other significant historical events would allow society to chart a different and more favorable course in the future.

Just as difficult as convincing students to realize the importance of studying history is the search for useful and interesting supplementary materials that present historical events in a context that can be easily understood. The volumes in Lucent Books' World History Series attempt to present a broad, balanced, and penetrating view of the march of history. Ancient Egypt's important wars and rulers, for example, are presented against the rich and colorful backdrop of Egyptian religious, social, and cultural developments. The series engages the reader by enhancing historical events with these cultural contexts. For example, in *Ancient Greece*, the text covers the role of women in that society. Slavery is discussed in *The Roman Empire*, as well as how slaves earned their freedom. The numerous and varied aspects of everyday life in these and other societies are explored in each volume of the series. Additionally, the series covers the major political, cultural, and philosophical ideas as the torch of civilization is passed from ancient Mesopotamia and Egypt, through Greece, Rome, Medieval Europe, and other world cultures, to the modern day.

The material in the series is formatted in a thorough, precise, and organized manner. Each volume offers the reader a comprehensive and clearly written overview of an important historical event or period. The topic under discussion is placed in a broad historical context. For example, *The Italian Renaissance* begins with a discussion of the High Middle Ages and the loss of central control that allowed certain Italian cities to develop artistically. The book ends by looking forward to the Reformation and interpreting the societal changes that grew out of the Renaissance. Thus, students are not only involved in an historical era, but also enveloped by the events leading up to that era and the events following it.

One important and unique feature in the World History Series is the primary and secondary source quotations that richly supplement each volume. These quotes are useful in a number of ways. First, they allow students access to sources they would not normally be exposed to because of the difficulty and obscurity of the original source. The quotations range from interesting anecdotes to farsighted cultural perspectives and are drawn from historical witnesses both past and present. Second, the quotes demonstrate how and where historians themselves derive their information on the past as they strive to reach a consensus on historical events. Lastly, all of the quotes are footnoted, familiarizing students with the citation process and allowing them to verify quotes and/or look up the original source if the quote piques their interest.

Finally, the books in the World History Series provide a detailed launching point for further research. Each book contains a bibliography specifically geared toward student research. A second, annotated bibliography introduces students to all the sources the author consulted when compiling the book. A chronology of important dates gives students an overview, at a glance, of the topic covered. Where applicable, a glossary of terms is included.

In short, the series is designed not only to acquaint readers with the basics of history, but also to make them aware that their lives are a part of an ongoing human saga. Perhaps they will then come to the same realization as famed historian Arnold Toynbee. In his monumental work, *A Study of History,* he wrote about becoming aware of history flowing through him in a mighty current, and of his own life "welling like a wave in the flow of this vast tide."

Important Dates in the History of the Black Death

1320s
Plague erupts in the Gobi Desert in central Asia

1346
Black Death reaches coast of the Black Sea

1347
Black Death reaches Constantinople

Fall 1347
Alexandria, Egypt, struck by Black Death

October 1347
Black Death reaches Europe for the first time at port of Messina, Sicily

Fall/Winter 1347
Florence, Italy, struck by Black Death; nearly sixty thousand die in a few months

December 1347
All southern Italy and much of southern Europe overcome by Black Death

Early 1348
Flagellant movement appears in Hungary

January 1348
Black Death strikes Pisa in northern Italy and port of Marseilles, France

February 1348
Black Death reaches Avignon, killing nearly half the population

April 1348
Many major inland cities of Italy struck by Black Death

Spring 1348
Black Death strikes Cairo, Egypt, where 200,000 die by fall; 60,000 die in city of Tunis in North Africa; pogroms against the Jews begin in France

May 1348
Black Death arrives in Pistoia and Siena, Italy; Paris struck by Black Death, killing one-third of the population by the winter of 1349

June 1348
Black Death crosses the Alps to Bavaria

July 1348
Black Death reaches Normandy in France, killing 30 percent of the population

August 1348
Black Death arrives in England through the port of Bristol

September 1348
London struck by Black Death, which lingers there until 1350 and kills 20,000 people; Pope Clement VI issues papal bull condemning the persecution of Jews

End of 1348
Black Death runs its course in Italy

Early 1349
Fringe elements take over flagellant movement

March 1349
England's West Midlands struck by Black Death

Spring 1349
Black Death reaches Ireland

May 1349
Scandinavia struck by Black Death

Summer 1349
Black Death reaches Tournai on border of Netherlands

July 1349
Scotland falls to Black Death

October 1349
Pope Clement VI issues papal bull calling for repression of flagellant movement

December 1349
Last pogrom associated with the Black Death occurs in Brussels

End of 1349
Black Death runs its course in Islamic world by the end of the year

1350
Flagellant movement almost completely disappears; Black Death spreads throughout Norway, Denmark, and Sweden

Spring 1350
Black Death arrives in Slavic Europe

January 1351
Black Death reaches easternmost edge of German-speaking Europe

End of 1351
Black Death disappears after coming full circle to the Russian steppe

The Spread of the Black Death in Europe

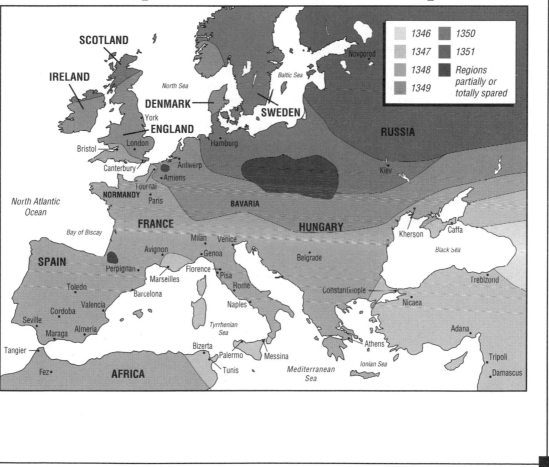

The Great Catastrophe

In the 1320s one of the most fearful and deadly diseases known to humans erupted from somewhere in central Asia. Slowly it began to spread to the east, to the south, and to the west. The disease took some twenty years—until 1347—to reach the island of Sicily, off the southern tip of Italy. It quickly reached Italy's many busy ports and then spread throughout Italy within months. In just four more years the dis-ease swept across Europe, killing about one-third of the population and in some areas as many as one-half or more of the people. It was the greatest natural catastrophe ever to strike Europe and one of the greatest catastrophes in world history. The disease reappeared ten years later, although not with the same ferocity, and it continued to recur regularly until the late seventeenth century. It struck at least once

An artist's depiction of the victims of Justinian's plague, in which 40 percent of the population died in Constantinople alone.

every generation during the century following its initial outbreak, and it was an important factor in the steady decline of the population of Europe. Historians estimate that European population declined between 60 and 75 percent during the century following 1349. At the time of its initial outbreak, it was known simply as the plague or the pestilence.

The plague had struck medieval Europe centuries before. The first pandemic (a widespread epidemic that recurs in cycles) appeared in A.D. 541 and is called Justinian's plague, after the Byzantine emperor of the time. In the Byzantine capital of Constantinople, the plague epidemic killed approximately 200,000 people—40 percent of the population—in a four-month span during 541–542. From Constantinople it swept across western Europe, reaching as far north as Denmark and as far west as Ireland. By the time Justinian's plague had run its course, it had killed approximately 20 to 25 percent of the entire population of Europe. Epidemics of the plague recurred in cycles every ten to twenty-four years for the following two hundred years. It was not until the late eighth century that the plague pandemic begun in Justinian's time finally came to an end.

Six hundred years later, the second plague pandemic of medieval times appeared, beginning with the great epidemic known as the Black Death. When the Black Death struck in the fourteenth century, Europe was far more populous than it had been during the first pandemic. Cities and towns were thriving all over the continent. Lands that had been covered with primeval forests and swampy marshes during the first pandemic were now cleared, drained, and cultivated by in-

A page from an illuminated manuscript depicts the plague's progression through a town. The main image depicts a burial scene; in the lower left hand corner are members of the royalty, afflicted by plague. Moving toward the lower right hand corner is death on horseback; moving up, monks attend a dying plague victim; and finally, monks perform a funeral service.

dustrious peasants. Europe was bursting with people—until the Black Death struck.

The number of dead the Black Death left in its wake was phenomenal—overall, at least one-third of the population of Europe. To put this number in modern terms, in 1990 the population of the United States was a little over 248 million. A loss of one-third of the population would mean that about 83 million people, or the equivalent of the entire combined populations of California, New York, Illinois, Ohio, and Texas, would die. If losses were spread evenly across the country, in every single classroom of thirty students, ten would die; in every family of four at least one parent or one child would be lost, and in many cases more than one family member would die. Everyone would lose someone—a parent, a grand-parent, a brother or sister, a friend.

To compound the horror of the Black Death, people of the time had no explana-tion or remedy for the terrible disease. Many people were convinced that it was a punishment from God, and thus they had an attitude of hopelessness in the face of death.

The Black Death touched every aspect of life—social, psychological, political, spiritual, intellectual, economic—and brought profound changes to medieval Europe. To all who lived through it, the Black Death was a time of almost unbeliev-able horror. As the Italian poet and hu-manist Petrarch wrote: "Oh happy posterity who will not experience such abysmal woe—and who will look upon our testimony as fable."[1]

Chapter

1 Europe Before the Black Death

The High Middle Ages, from approximately A.D. 1000 to 1300, was an era of growing peace and prosperity in Europe. By the eleventh century, invasions by Slavic and Norse marauders had ended. By the mid–thirteenth century, Mongol invasions in the east had stopped. Kings had grown in power, ending much of the raiding by rival nobles and increasing political stability. Although knights still carried on petty wars and local raids, Europe was free from major wars for most of the thirteenth century.

Political stability encouraged economic and social stability. As the population grew, more and more farmland was

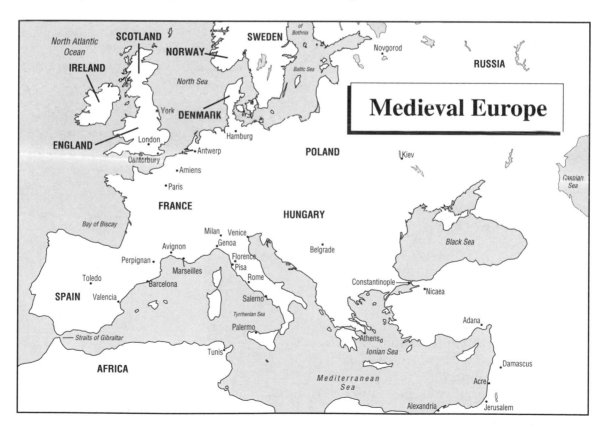

Every individual in medieval society had a place under feudalism. Here, peasants tend to their lord's manor. These peasants would probably never go more than ten miles from the manor in their entire lives.

Feudalism

By the 1300s, the feudal system that had governed the Middle Ages was beginning to break down. With the rise of trade and a merchant class, money, rather than land, became an important economic factor. The services of knights could be paid for in cash rather than land, and feudal relationships weakened. Further, the heavily armored, mounted knight was becoming obsolete in the face of new methods of warfare: Gunpowder came into use, and castles could not stand against cannon. Longbowmen, whose powerful weapons could pierce armor, routed French knights at the Battle of Crécy in 1346 and introduced the longbow as a potent new weapon of war. The decline of feudalism in the face of these forces was inevitable, but it was hastened by the Black Death, which appeared a year after the Battle of Crécy.

A king receives a knight. Knights agreed to pledge loyalty and military aid to a king in exchange for land and a title.

needed. Fortunately, an unusual period of warm weather helped ensure rich harvests ample enough to feed the growing population. The warm climate allowed people to cultivate crops and graze animals on marginal lands that in later centuries were too cold for agricultural use. The increase in arable land plus the absence of serious epidemics allowed the population to triple from about 25 million in A.D. 950 to 75 million in the year 1250.

Trade and commerce were growing fast. Magnificent stone cathedrals rose across the face of Europe, symbols of the deep spiritual commitment of medieval Christians. European civilization was again on the rise.

The Serfs of God

Prior to the thirteenth century, many freemen willingly gave themselves and their descendants up to serfdom, supposedly as an act of devotion to God but in reality to receive a land grant. In The Making of the Middle Ages, *historian R. W. Southern quotes an eleventh-century document that details one such sacrifice.*

"Be it known to all who come after us, that a certain man in our service called William, the brother of Reginald, born of free parents, being moved by the love of God and to the end that God . . . might look favorably on him, gave himself up as a serf to St. Martin of Marmoutier; and he gave not only himself but all his descendants, so that they should for ever serve the abbot and monks of this place in a servile condition."

This miniature from an Anglo-Saxon manuscript depicts peasants plowing their lord's land.

Manorialism

From the fall of the Roman Empire through the Middle Ages, European society existed under the social and economic system of manorialism. Manors were large estates controlled by lords. Most manors consisted of a manor house, or on larger estates a castle, surrounded by gardens, orchards, and fields and included a mill for grinding grain into flour, a press for making wine, and a church. Manors were self-sufficient social and economic units, providing the necessities of life for their inhabitants.

About 90 percent of the people of Europe were peasants who lived under the manorial system and were bound to the land as serfs. The land they worked on and on which their villages stood was controlled by the lords or often by the clergy, the heads of great abbeys, who were the landlords. The peasants were tied to the land they worked. If control of the land changed hands, the peasants were bound to the new landlord. Peasants could not legally move to a city or another manor; they rarely traveled far from the place of their birth.

Peasants' lives were difficult. They paid rent to the landlord for the lands they farmed for themselves, and they paid rent for their houses and gardens. Prior to the middle of the twelfth century, peasants paid their rent in food or other goods, but later many began to pay rent in cash from what they earned by selling food to the growing number of town and city dwellers. In addition to rent, peasants were obliged to provide free labor on the demesne, or lands used by the lord. Crops

A tenant pays rent to the lord of the manor. Although peasants' lives were difficult, they had a permanent place to live and protection against roving bandits and rival lords.

An early architectural plan shows the layout of a manor. The manor was completely self-sufficient.

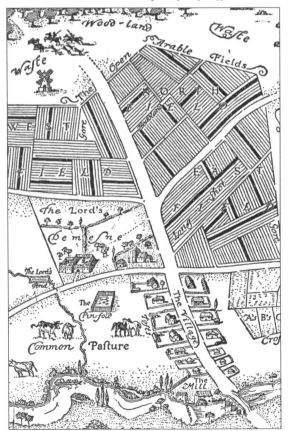

from the demesne belonged to the lord. Peasants also owed extra work on the demesne during the harvest. An even heavier burden was the tithe, or 10 percent of their crops or their earnings, which went to the church. Finally, there was the heriot, or tribute owed to the landlord upon the death of the peasant, in theory to repay the landlord for labor lost. At the death of the head of the household, just at the time when a family was in most need, peasants were forced to surrender their best animal, or some other valuable, to their lord.

On the other hand, peasants did benefit from the manorial system. They were guaranteed a permanent place to live and work for themselves and their descendants. The lord offered protection from enemies, and the peasants felt a bond of personal loyalty to the lord of the manor.

By the 1300s the manorial system, like the feudal system, was breaking down. The increase in trade and industry enabled people to pay for goods and services with cash. Enterprising serfs were able to buy themselves out of serfdom. As the population grew, the lords were anxious to increase arable lands, and peasants obtained freedom from labor obligations through *assarting*—clearing previously uncultivated

Peasant and Lord

In his book The Civilization of the Middle Ages, *historian Norman Cantor describes the place of the peasants and the lords at the end of the thirteenth century.*

"A traveler through the European countryside in 1300 would have found much the same conditions of intensive cultivation and rural prosperity that exist there today. There was a thriving market for grain, mutton and beef, wool, and grapes for wine, and landlords took pains to get the largest possible yield from their estates. The more enlightened were well aware of the advantages of manure for fertilizer and the rudiments of animal husbandry. The peasant, fast moving out of his servile status, was becoming either a rent-paying free tenant or a small landowner himself. Sir Walter of Henley, an English gentleman of the mid–thirteenth century, remarked in a treatise on successful farming that 'great wealth' will come to those who 'know how to keep all the points of husbandry, as the tillage of land and the keeping of cattle.' The petty lord or country gentleman, smelling of the barn and fields, and the ambitious peasant, squeezing every possible ounce of profit from his land, were central figures in European rural society and have remained so, especially in France, down to the present day, while the captains and kings have come and gone.

In 1300, however, the great lords—the high nobility—still dominated rural Europe. In all countries their castles and chateaus loomed triumphant on the horizon. The booming agricultural market and the favors gained at the royal court enriched the aristocracy as never before, while literacy and the chivalric code gave them a heightened consciousness of their superior status. The great lords looked down upon the simple country gentleman with arrogant disdain."

lands for the lords. Peasants, who had at least partially freed themselves by clearing the lands, still owed rent on these lands, but they had no labor or other obligations to the lord. In other cases, particularly in northeastern Europe, peasants drained swamps and cleared primeval forests at the frontiers of civilization. Many lords preferred to "farm out" all of their lands, taking cash payment from the peasants who farmed their demesne, rather than taking peasant labor in payment.

In the years just before the arrival of the Black Death, the old manorial system was undergoing fundamental changes. Landlords commonly paid cash instead of land for some goods and services from peasants and craftsmen; in turn, landlords often received cash rents for their lands rather than services from peasants. Peasants, who felt the squeeze of more and more people onto small pieces of land, often simply ran away to cities or towns. Although it was still illegal for serfs to leave the land, the landlords did little to stop them because peasant laborers were plentiful.

The Church

During the High Middle Ages, the Roman Church was the only form of Christianity. It occupied a central role in European society and in the lives of individuals, in part because it was probably the most powerful and wealthiest landowner in Europe. Ideally, the clergy's function was to maintain the spiritual well-being of society through prayer and good works. Since members of the clergy were likely to be literate and well educated, they also functioned as clerks and bureaucrats.

Much like the nobility, the church had a hierarchy of important posts. At the top was the pope, whose residence was in Rome and who had authority over all the clergy of the church. Archbishops ruled over a wide area, or archdiocese, comprised of several dioceses ruled by the next level in the hierarchy, the bishops. Next in importance were abbots, who controlled monasteries or abbeys, and under abbots were monks and village priests. Village priests were often as poor as their

A Prayer for Food

During the famines of the early 1300s, many people turned to God, as chronicler Guillaume de Nages, quoted in Robert Gottfried's The Black Death, *describes.*

"We saw a large number of both sexes, not only from nearby places but from as much as five leagues away, barefooted and maybe even, except for women, in a completely nude state, together with their priests coming in procession at the Church of the Holy Martyrs, their bones bulging out, devoutly carrying bodies of saints and other relics to be adored, hoping to get relief."

The church had much invested in the feudal system, for it was the largest landholder in Europe. In this drawing, all levels of the church hierarchy are depicted, from the pope to village priests. People affected with the plague stand in the lower right hand corner, foreshadowing the end of the church's iron grip on society.

peasants, but monks were often quite comfortable in their abbeys. An abbey often had a great deal of land attached to it and functioned much like a manor house, making the abbot quite wealthy from the labor of his peasants.

Since the church owned so much land, it had an interest in maintaining the status quo—the feudal and manorial systems—and preached that the power of the aristocrats and the church, and the poverty of the peasants, was God's plan. According to Gerard, an eleventh-century bishop, "From the beginning, mankind has been divided into three parts, among men of prayer, farmers, and men of war."[2] Peasants, who were almost universally illiterate, meekly accepted their suffering on earth and looked forward to their reward in heaven.

The Trifunctional Society

The three important players in medieval European society—the nobility or warrior class, the church, and the peasantry—make up what historians call the trifunctional society. The trifunctional society was first mentioned about the year 1000 by Adalbero, a nobleman and descendant of Charlemagne, who wrote: "Here below, some pray, others fight, and still others work."[3] Despite the unfair distribution of wealth and the suffering of the peasants, for centuries the trifunctional society had provided a stable, harmonious social order. By the 1300s, many factors were contributing to its disintegration, but the Black Death hastened these changes and helped to end the medieval way of life.

Rural Life

Under the manorial system, villages of the manor were self-sufficient. Craftsmen such as carpenters, millers, and blacksmiths, who produced the goods needed by the village, were not bound serfs and were paid for their labor. The peasants spent their days working on small strips of land granted to them by the lord of the manor, as well as working on the lord's demesne. At sundown they returned to their small, windowless huts made of wood or mud, with thatched roofs and dirt floors. Their furniture was sparse, with rough stools or benches and a table. The entire family usually slept in one room on beds of straw, and they often shared their huts with their farm animals. The huts had no fireplaces, and in the winter peasants built fires on the dirt floor for warmth. Food was often scarce in the winter.

The lord of the manor and his family and servants lived a much more comfortable life. The manor home was often spacious, with rich furnishings and large stone fireplaces.

As a medieval potter works, peasants labor in the fields in the background. It took the work of many craftsmen and laborers to make the manor self-sufficient.

Life in Towns and Cities

Most medieval towns were small by today's standards, only a few thousand people— small urban islands scattered across the immense rural landscape of Europe. A few urban centers were truly cities: London, Paris, and Florence all boasted populations of 50,000 to 100,000.

Since many towns were surrounded by massive walls—a legacy of earlier times built as protection from the raids of warring nobles—they were cramped. The streets were narrow, and houses had two, three, or four stories.

Like all aspects of medieval life, urban areas were changing, growing in response to the growing population and the greater opportunities for freedom that peasants enjoyed. Unskilled peasants left their lords' manors and their serfdom behind, hoping for a better life in the towns. They believed in the medieval saying, "Urban air makes free." Unfortunately they found that there was little need for unskilled labor in the towns. Small merchants and craftsmen such as masons, carpenters, and tailors could make a comfortable living in towns, but the unskilled peasants were usually forced to survive on odd jobs such as cleaning stables or loading and unloading wagons.

Swelling populations made urban life overcrowded and unsanitary. Drunken rowdies were an everyday annoyance. Fires caused by open fireplaces that ignited thatch roofs and wooden buildings were commonplace. Nevertheless, in 1173 William Fitz-Stephen, writing a "chamber of commerce" advertisement for London, claimed that in London "the only pests . . . are the immoderate drinking of fools and frequency of fires."[4] People endured the inconveniences because towns still offered great economic and cultural opportunities.

Although the streets in the center of medieval towns were often cobblestoned, most other streets were unpaved, narrow, dirt paths. They were muddy most of the time, and open gutters carried human waste out of town to the nearest river. The stench was overpowering. Garbage lay rotting in the streets, where dogs, pigs, and the ever-present black rats foraged.

A notable exception to the generally unsanitary medieval towns was the town of Nuremberg in Germany. There the paved streets were cleaned regularly, trash was carted out of town, and pigs were not allowed to roam free. Even personal cleanliness was considered important: Nuremberg had fourteen public baths, and workers were given money to pay the cost of bathing as part of their wages. Cleanliness paid off. When the Black Death struck, Nuremberg had the lowest death toll of any European city.

However, most medieval towns were not like Nuremberg. The dirty narrow streets housed the peasant laborers, while the cobblestoned streets in the center of town were lined with the comfortable houses of merchants and master craftsmen. Shops occupied the ground floors of

Florence during the Middle Ages. Although this romanticized painting does not reveal it, Florence was just as overcrowded, filthy, and unsanitary as other medieval towns.

these structures, and the family lived in the upper floors, along with their apprentices and servants.

Craftsmen and tradespeople of medieval times had formed themselves into guilds, similar to modern-day labor unions. Anyone who wanted to practice a trade had to belong to a guild. The guilds controlled the price and quality of goods, who could become guild members, and what wages guild members received. Guild members often occupied important positions on the town council.

Guilds thrived throughout Europe. Stonemasons were in heavy demand to build the grand cathedrals and churches. Bakers, carpenters, glassblowers, weavers, and other textile workers were among the many craftsmen who were kept busy by the burgeoning European economy.

A street scene depicts medieval craftsmen selling wares and performing services such as barbering. The development of a craftsman class, through guilds, eroded the feudal system.

On market days, merchants and craftsmen erected colorful tents and stalls from which to sell their cloth, ribbons, knives, swords, baked goods, spices, and other wares. Traveling musicians, jugglers, and dancing bears crowded the streets.

Crusaders returning from the Holy Land after the great crusades of the eleventh and twelfth centuries had brought back a taste for the spices and luxury items of the Near East, and as the population and wealth of towns increased, there was a greater demand for imported goods. Italian merchants in port cities grew wealthy acting as middlemen, importing goods from the East and passing them on to other European cities where they were sold in the marketplaces or at fairs.

The Italian cities of Genoa, Pisa, and Venice sent out their own fleets in the Mediterranean to safeguard their trade routes. Other Italian cities became prosperous banking centers, financing the treasuries of kings and the trading voyages of merchant ships. There was a growing need for capital—cash money used to expand a business—and Italian bankers grew wealthy filling this need by lending businesspeople money.

In the prosperous cities of northern Italy, many of the rich bourgeoisie, or middle class, invested their money in public works. Historian Norman Cantor explains:

> High bourgeois families, grown fabulously rich from commerce and banking, imitated . . . the French aristocratic style. Freeing themselves of the smell of warehouse and counting-house, they became the first urban aristocracy in Europe since the heyday of the Roman Empire. Civic pride in-

An Italian merchant boasts the clothing of a wealthy man. Because it was a center of trade, Italy was an especially profitable nation for merchants, who acted as buyers and sellers of goods.

spired them to adorn their cities with public buildings, squares, and monuments that provided a worthy setting for their own palazzos [mansions].[5]

By the 1300s, European trade and commerce was thriving. Italian merchants brought trade goods from the East and found enthusiastic buyers in the marketplaces of the growing towns and cities of Europe.

A Deceptive Quiet

Europeans looked to the future optimistically as the fourteenth century approached. A general state of peace had settled over Europe. The old feudal and manorial systems were breaking down, and peasants were gaining more freedom.

Towns were growing, trade was increasing, and many people were improving their lot in life. Children born at the turn of the fourteenth century seemed to face a life of promise. No one could have guessed that those children who would grow to maturity would experience one of the most crisis-ridden centuries in history. Historian Denys Hay sums up the situation in Europe at the close of the thirteenth century.

> The clearing of the forests, the eastward extension of more advanced methods of cultivation of the soil, the renewed exploitation of mineral wealth, the development of specialized crafts and of international trade, all suggest that the economic condition of Europe as a whole was still improving at the end of the thirteenth century. It was a moment when the burden of serfdom was disappearing from western Europe and when it had not yet fallen heavily on the countries of the north-eastern plain. It is possible that the lot of the peasants was never happier than it was at this time. There was a blessed [end of] barbarian invasion after those of the Mongols in the mid–thirteenth century. Wars were still local and short and Europe in the thirteenth century enjoyed relative peace and prosperity. Soon economic regression was to come. The great famine of 1317, the Hundred Years' War, the Turks and the Black Death arrived to put an end to what had been a [golden] time.[6]

The Crises Begin

About 1250 the climate of Europe slowly began to change, growing colder and

Farmers harvest wheat during the Middle Ages. In the early 1300s, much of the wheat crop was failing, and many people went hungry.

wetter. The decade of the 1290s was extremely wet, causing crop failures in various parts of Europe. By 1300 most of the marginal land was failing, barely able to

A peasant shears a sheep in the shadow of the manor house. When the deadly animal disease murrain began to reach epidemic proportions in 1317, it led to further starvation as many sheep fell victim to the disease.

sustain crops. To make matters worse, much of the land was given over to wheat farming, since wheat was the most profitable crop. However, in a bad year for wheat many people went hungry because there were few alternative sources of grain.

As long as the crop failures were localized, urban and rural areas could import grain from parts of Europe where crops had been good. But Europe entered a "little Ice Age" in which the climate became colder and wetter, the growing season became shorter, and crop failures were commonplace. During the great famine of 1315–1317, one of the worst of the century, agriculture all over Europe suffered. Urban areas which had a concentration of people and had to import large amounts of grain were the hardest hit. In Ypres, Flanders (now called Belgium), approximately 20 percent of the town's population of about twenty-eight thousand had died by 1317. Even though the large cities had made provisions for food shortages, they suffered terribly.

Many historians believe that the terrible famines of the first half of the fourteenth century were partly responsible for the high death rates during the Black Death. People had been malnourished for a generation and were more susceptible to disease.

The harvests improved somewhat after 1317, but another catastrophe struck. Cattle and sheep began to die from an epidemic of murrain, a highly contagious and deadly animal disease. Livestock herds all over Europe were drastically depleted, which was an especially heavy burden for wool-producing areas.

Not only peasants were affected by agricultural failures and destruction of livestock. The crisis gradually began to affect all commercial activity, as food costs soared and people had less money to spend on luxury items.

The aristocracy who depended on the land for wealth continued to prosper despite the agricultural crisis. Crop yields decreased, but population continued to grow; thus the demand for land—and the rent for it—continued to rise. Peasants whose land was producing less and less were faced with increased rent costs; large landholders prospered while the peasants suffered. However, the aristocracy faced other serious problems as their traditional role in society gradually became outmoded. According to author Robert Gottfried:

> New weapons and methods of military organization challenged the nobility's supremacy on the battlefield. Mercenary armies, using pikes and longbows, took the measure of knights in the field, while artillery in the hands of kings threatened knights in their castles. . . . There were no more infidel or pagan armies, save in parts of southeastern and far eastern Christendom, from whom the lords had to protect the peasants; indeed, to many peasants, it was the lords who represented the greatest threat to stability and security.[7]

People had still another terrible hardship to endure—the Hundred Years' War

Rioting for Food

Europeans suffered severely from the famine of the early 1300s. In Italy, famine-stricken rioters were sternly punished, as the Florentine chronicler Giovanni Villani describes in Robert Gottfried's The Black Death.

"The famine was felt not only in Florence but throughout Tuscany and Italy. And so terrible was it that the Perugians, the Sienese, the Lucchese, the Pistolese and many other townsmen drove from their territory all their beggars because they could not support them. . . . The agitation of the [Florentine] people at the market of San Michele was so great that it was necessary to protect officials by means of guards fitted out with an axe and block to punish rioters on the spot with the loss of their hands and their feet."

In addition to poor harvests and devastating disease, another factor that led to the starvation and death of many peasants was the Hundred Years' War between England and France.

between France and England. Begun in 1337, the war was a series of intermittent but devastating invasions of France by English forces. As English armies moved through France, they looted towns and villages of food and other valuables. As a defense, the French armies practiced a scorched-earth policy in their own countryside, burning everything that could be of use to the English invaders. French peasants suffered equally at the hands of the English and the French.

As 1347 approached, the old bonds of European society between nobles and peasants were gradually beginning to break down. People of Europe were exhausted from the extended agricultural crisis and a decade of war. But the most devastating crisis of all was about to strike—the Black Death.

2 The Black Death Begins

Historians believe that the deadly microbe that caused the Black Death originated in central Asia. The bacilli, known today as *Yersinia pestis*, is carried in the bellies of fleas that live on rodents. Normally, the bacilli live comfortably in the stomach of the flea, causing little trouble. However, for reasons still unknown to science, during the Black Death epidemic the plague bacilli began to multiply rapidly, blocking the flea's stomach and causing it to starve. While feeding, the flea regurgitated *Y. pestis* bacilli into the bloodstream of its host. As the hosts died, the starving fleas quickly found new hosts. They preferred rodents—the ground-dwelling rodents of central Asia, or the common black rat of medieval Europe—but as a last resort, they fed on human hosts, infecting them with the plague bacilli.

Central Asia was sparsely populated during the fourteenth century, but it was the center of a sprawling Mongol empire founded by Genghis Khan and encompassing a vast area that included all of China, much of Russia, and what is now Iran and Iraq. The headquarters of the Mongol empire was Karakoam in the Gobi Desert. From there the Mongols maintained a communications network that linked China, Russia, India, the Middle East, and the trade routes that led to Eu-rope. Trade between the East and the West was thriving in the early fourteenth century. The luxury goods of China and

Merchants travel through central Asia. Historians believe the Black Death was spread by Mongol messengers or armies that traveled from China to the Middle East.

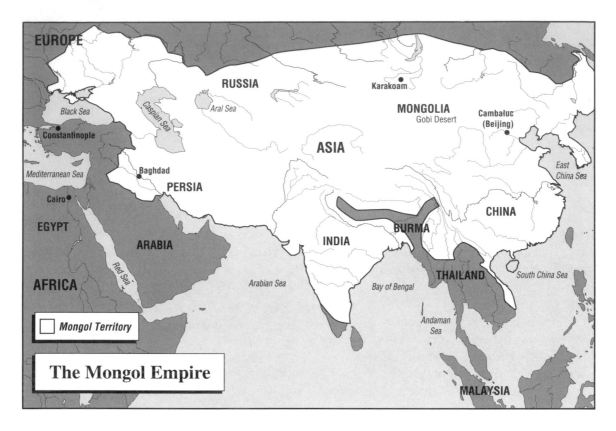

☐ *Mongol Territory*

EUROPE

RUSSIA

Karakoam

Black Sea

Caspian Sea

Aral Sea

MONGOLIA
Gobi Desert

Cambaluc
(Beijing)

Constantinople

ASIA

Mediterranean Sea

Baghdad

PERSIA

East
China Sea

Cairo

CHINA

EGYPT

ARABIA

INDIA

BURMA

Red Sea

Arabian Sea

Bay of Bengal

THAILAND

South China Sea

AFRICA

Andaman
Sea

MALAYSIA

the Spice Islands were brought to markets in Europe via three major trade routes from China, India, and the Middle East to trading centers on the northern shore of the Black Sea and to ports on the Mediterranean and the Nile River. From these trading centers and ports, Italian merchants transported goods by ship to ports in Italy and southern France and then overland to northern Europe. The infected fleas and rodents may have been carried by Mongol messengers, who could travel as far as one hundred miles a day on horseback for weeks at a time. Possibly the infected hosts were carried by Mongol armies and their supply trains that crisscrossed the empire and the caravans that traveled the ancient Silk Road from China to the Middle East. During the height of Mongol power (1279–1350), the thousands of people who were traveling across Eurasia were all potential carriers of the deadly fleas and rodents.

The Plague in the East

Sometime in the late 1320s, plague erupted in the Gobi Desert and slowly spread across Asia. Records recounting the southward and eastward movement of the plague are sketchy for that time, but historians believe the plague reached China in 1331. Asia was already reeling under a series of natural disasters—droughts, earthquakes, floods, swarms of locusts—which had caused widespread famine. The plague was a deadly blow to an already weakened nation. Coupled with other natural disasters, the plague killed two-thirds of the population of China between 1331 and 1353, when the first reliable chronicles of the time were written.

By 1346 the plague had reached westward to the Caucasus and Azerbaijan along the coast of the Black Sea. Rumors of its devastation in the east had reached ports in the Mediterranean, and one chronicler of the time reports:

> India was depopulated; Tartary [a vast region that includes present-day northern China, Mongolia, and southern Russia], Mesopotamia, Syria, Armenia were covered with dead bodies; the Kurds fled in vain to the mountains. In Caramania and Caesaria [in Asia Minor] none were left alive.[8]

Rumors of floods, earthquakes, famine, and plague in the East reached Europe. However, the majority of Europeans, especially peasants, rarely traveled beyond their villages, and these places—China, India, the Middle East—were remote. The average European, tending his crops and animals or selling his wares in the marketplace, never dreamed that similar disasters would strike him.

By 1347 the Black Death reached Constantinople, capital of the Byzantine empire. For centuries, Constantinople had been an important trading center, controlling the passage between the Black Sea and the Mediterranean. In 1347 Constantinople was a city with a population of between 100,000 and 250,000. One observer of the plague in Constantinople, a trader from Venice, claimed that 90 percent of the people died. That was surely an exaggeration, but his testimony illustrates that, for the people who lived through the epidemic, it must have seemed like the world had ended.

War and Pestilence in China

Little information exists about the Black Death in China. However, records do indicate a dramatic drop in population. Historians believe that this was caused by the Black Death, as William McNeill discusses in his book Plagues and Peoples.

"The combination of war [against Mongol domination] and pestilence wreaked havoc on China's population. The best estimates show a decrease from 123 million about 1200 (before the Mongol invasions began) to a mere 65 million in 1393, a generation after the final expulsion of the Mongols from China. Even Mongol ferocity cannot account for such a drastic decrease. Disease assuredly played a big part in cutting Chinese numbers in half; and bubonic plague, recurring after its initial ravages at relatively frequent intervals, just as in Europe, is by all odds the most likely candidate for such a role."

An ancient drawing of Constantinople. The plague decimated the population of Constantinople in 1347.

The Plague in the Muslim World

In the fall of 1347, Italian merchants carried the plague into the Muslim world. Alexandria, a city of 100,000, sitting at the edge of the Nile River delta, was the principal Mediterranean port of Egypt. At its peak in Alexandria, the Black Death killed up to 750 a day.

The Black Death then moved up the Nile River, devastating villages in the Nile delta. Gardens were left untended, daily business stopped, and bodies piled up for lack of people to bury them. In some

God Inherits the Earth

In this quote, taken from Robert Gottfried's book The Black Death, *Muslim historian Ibn Khaldun, whose parents perished in the plague, wrote of the plague's aftermath in the Islamic world.*

"Civilization both in the East and the West was visited by a destructive plague which devastated nations and caused populations to vanish. It swallowed up many of the good things of civilization and wiped them out. It overtook dynasties at the time of their senility, when they had reached the limit of their duration. It lessened their power and curtailed their influence. It weakened their authority. Their situation approached the point of annihilation and dissolution. Civilization decreased with the decrease of mankind. Cities and buildings were laid waste, roads and way signs were obliterated, settlements and mansions became empty, and dynasties and tribes grew weak. The entire inhabited world changed. . . . It was as if the voice of existence in the world had called out for oblivion and restriction and the world responded to its call. God inherits the earth and whoever is upon it."

cases, bodies were stacked so high along the roadside that bandits hid behind them to ambush travelers.

In the spring of 1348, the Black Death reached one of the world's largest cities, Cairo, Egypt, with a population of about 500,000. In all, 200,000 citizens of Cairo died, nearly 40 percent of the city's population and more than the entire population of most Christian cities of the time.

The plague continued to spread throughout the Middle East, to Palestine and across the Arabian Peninsula, striking even in Mecca, the holiest city of Islam. By 1349 the Black Death had swept through the entire Islamic world. The plague had come so quickly and destroyed so many that the survivors were left in shock.

In all, about one-third of the population of the Islamic world perished. While the Muslim world staggered under the fierce attack of plague, the disease was also crippling the West.

The Black Death Reaches Italy

According to a traditional story, the plague came to Europe from the town of Caffa, a Crimean port on the Black Sea where Italian merchants from Genoa maintained a thriving trade center. The Crimea was inhabited by Tartars, a people of the steppe, a dry, treeless region of central Asia. When the plague struck the area in 1346, tens of thousands of Tartars died. Perhaps superstition caused the Muslim Tartars to blame their misfortune on the Christian Genoese. Or perhaps it was because a Christian and a Muslim had become involved in a street brawl in Caffa, and the Tartars wanted revenge. In any case, the Tartars sent an army to attack Caffa, where the Genoese had fortified themselves. As the Tartars laid siege to Caffa, plague struck their army and many

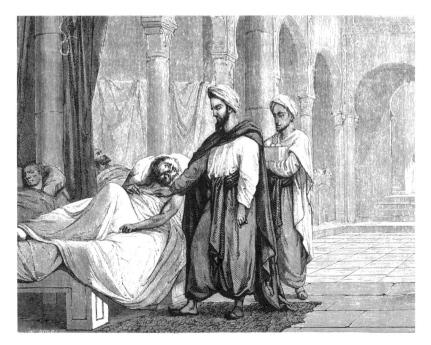

A plague victim is nursed in a medieval Moorish hospital. The Black Death reached Cairo, Egypt, in 1348 and left about 200,000 people dead.

died. The Tartars decided to share their suffering with the Genoese. They used huge catapults to lob the infected corpses of plague victims over the walls of Caffa. As the Tartars had intended, the rotting corpses littered the streets, and the plague quickly spread throughout the besieged city. The Genoese decided they must flee; they boarded their galleys and set sail for Italy, carrying rats, fleas, and the Black Death with them.

Although this traditional story of how the Black Death came to Europe may not be true in all its particulars—or it may not be true at all—it is certain that the rats that spread the Black Death traveled to

A Tartar warrior on horseback. Legend has it that the Black Death reached Caffa when the Tartars catapulted the plague-infected corpses of their dead over Caffa's city walls.

Europe on merchant ships from the eastern Mediterranean, and the disease probably reached many ports at about the same time. Italy, being the trading center for Europe, was the hardest hit, since Italian merchant ships docked in dozens of Italian ports.

The first wave of the Black Death came in early October 1347, when a fleet of twelve Genoese merchant ships sailed into the harbor of Messina, a town on the island of Sicily, off the southern tip of Italy. According to Michael of Piazza, a chronicler of the time, the entire crew had "sickness clinging to their very bones."[9] Frantic harbormasters turned the ships away, but they were too late. The ships had docked long enough to allow rats carrying infected fleas to go ashore. As the rat hosts died, infected fleas quickly found new hosts, many of whom were human. Within a few days, the plague had spread throughout Messina. In Messina, hundreds were dying daily. Panicked citizens began fleeing to the countryside, carrying the sickness with them. Some reached the town of Catania, a port city some distance from Messina. The Genoese fleet was driven away, only to carry the disease to other ports in the Mediterranean.

At first, citizens of Catania treated the people of Messina kindly, even caring for them in the hospital. But when they realized the deadliness of the disease, they began to control immigration. According to Michael of Piazza, the Catanians "refused even to speak to any from Messina, or to have anything to do with them, but quickly fled at their approach."[10] As was the case everywhere the Black Death struck, quarantine and avoidance of the sick did little to help. By the end of October, Catania was overwhelmed with the

Visions of Evil

Fear and superstition colored many of the eyewitness accounts of the plague. According to the chronicler Michael of Piazza, when the patriarch archbishop of Catania visited Messina hoping to relieve the suffering, he was greeted by an evil vision. This quote is taken from Philip Ziegler's book The Black Death.

"The aforesaid Patriarch landed at Messina carrying with him the holy water . . . and in that city there appeared demons transfigured into the shape of dogs, who wrought grievous harm upon the bodies of the citizens; so that men were aghast and dared not go forth from their houses. Yet by common consent, and at the wish of the Archbishop, they determined to march devoutly around the city reciting litanies. While the whole population was thus processing around the streets, a black dog, bearing a drawn sword in his paws, appeared among them, gnashing with his teeth and rushing upon them and breaking all the silver vessels and lamps and candlesticks on the altars, and casting them hither and thither. . . . So the people of Messina, terrified by this prodigious vision, were all strangely overcome by fear."

disease. By November, all of Sicily had succumbed. By December, the Black Death had engulfed all of southern Italy and much of southern Europe.

The Plague in Florence

Florence was one of Italy's most prosperous and beautiful cities. The great merchant and banking families of Florence had amassed enormous wealth, which they lavished on public buildings and works of art.

When the plague reached Florence late in 1347, its citizens had already been weakened by a famine that had afflicted most of Italy. Of the city's approximately eighty thousand inhabitants, about four

thousand died immediately. Then the plague seemed to diminish during that winter, but in the spring of 1348 it struck again with a renewed fury.

Florence was the home of the great writer and humanist Giovanni Boccaccio, who wrote a lengthy and famous account of the Black Death in his city. According to Boccaccio, many of the wealthy deserted the city for their country estates while the plague raged. Those left, primarily the poor, suffered terribly:

Being confined to their own parts of the city, they fell ill daily in their thousands, and since they had no one to assist them or attend to their needs, they inevitably perished almost without exception. Many dropped dead in the

Priests tend to plague victims in Italy. So many died that priests were unable to perform services for all of the dead.

horrible odor. The victim suffered severe pain and died within five days. A terrible despair and depression preceded death, as the disease affected the nervous system, and one chronicler claimed that as the victim neared his end "death is seen seated on the face."

The fear and horror of the disease was so great that normal human ties broke down, and many people were left to die alone as Boccaccio describes:

> It was not merely a question of one citizen avoiding another, and of people almost invariably neglecting their neighbours and rarely or never visiting their relatives, addressing them only from a distance; this scourge had implanted so great a terror in the hearts of men and women that brothers abandoned brothers, uncles their nephews, sisters their brothers, and in many cases wives deserted their husbands. But even worse, and almost incredible, was the fact that fathers and mothers refused to nurse and assist their own children, as though they did not belong to them.[12]

Plague often wiped out entire families, and the number of dead was so great that people became numb to the sight of death. Boccaccio describes funeral processions in which two or three or more family members were placed on one bier:

> Times without number it happened that two priests would be on their way to bury someone . . . only to find that bearers carrying three or four additional biers would fall in behind them. . . . Even in these circumstances, however, there were no tears or candles or mourners to honor the dead; in fact,

open streets, both by day and by night, whilst a great many others, though dying in their own houses, drew their neighbours' attention to the fact more by the smell of their rotting corpses than by any other means. And what with these, and the others who were dying all over the city, bodies were here, there and everywhere.[11]

People who watched family members and friends die were understandably horrified. Plague victims suffered a terrible end. The first symptoms were egg-size black swellings, or buboes (hence the name bubonic), under the armpits and in the groin. Then purplish blotches caused by hemorrhaging under the skin appeared. The buboes sometimes burst, oozing blood and pus. A terrible stench was associated with the disease—the victim's blood, breath, sweat, and urine all had a no more respect was accorded to dead people than would nowadays be shown towards dead goats.[13]

In Florence, as elsewhere, burying the dead became the most immediate problem, as Boccaccio describes:

> When all the graves were full, huge trenches were excavated in the churchyards, into which new arrivals were placed in their hundreds, stowed tier upon tier like ships' cargo, each layer of corpses being covered over with a thin layer of soil till the trench was filled to the top.[14]

The horror of the Black Death brought out the best and the worst in people. As the dead died faster than the living could bury them, families simply placed their dead out in front of their doorway. Every morning, a religious group known as the Compagnia della Misericordia, which had been founded a century earlier to care for the sick, collected the corpses. The members of the order were noted for their distinctive dress—red robes and hoods that covered them head to toe; even their faces were covered so that only their eyes showed. But the number of dead was overwhelming, and corpses sometimes lay piled up in the streets for days at a time, putrefying and spreading further disease, despite efforts to collect them.

In contrast to the charity of the Compagnia della Misericordia was the ruthlessness of the *becchini*. These people, who were often themselves dying of the plague, charged outrageous fees to cart away the dead and often performed tasks no one else would do. They also broke into homes of the sick, threatening to carry away the healthy if their demands were not met. They stole whatever they wished, and they assaulted, raped, and even murdered citizens. Since so many of the law enforcement officials had died of the plague, the *becchini* were free to roam the city streets. As Boccaccio describes:

> In the face of so much affliction and misery, all respect for the laws of God and man had virtually broken down

Plague victims display the swollen, egg-size buboes that were characteristic of the plague. In the background, a priest or sorcerer attempts a primitive cure.

and been extinguished in our city. For like everybody else, those ministers and executors of the laws who were not either dead or ill were left with so few subordinates that they were unable to discharge any of their duties. Hence everyone was free to behave as he pleased.[15]

The plague spread rapidly through Florence, and within a few months one-third of the residents had died. The overwhelming number of deaths caused a crisis of another kind. Factories and shops were closed: There were few workers to operate them, and those who were left feared contact with others. As workers died, the system that in normal times brought goods from the countryside collapsed. Prices of food and other necessities soared.

Boccaccio claimed that 100,000 Florentines died of the plague—a certain exaggeration, since the population at the time was only about 80,000. Nevertheless, of all the great cities, Florence was the hardest hit by the plague. Before the Black Death was finished, possibly as much as 75 percent of the population had died—an astonishing 60,000 people.

Funerals of the Black Death

In his book The Decameron, *Italian author and humanist Giovanni Boccaccio, who was an eyewitness to the Black Death, describes how funeral customs in Florence broke down during the plague.*

"It had once been customary . . . for the women relatives and neighbours of a dead man to assemble in his house in order to mourn in the company of the women who had been closest to him; moreover his kinsfolk would [gather] in front of his house along with his neighbours and various other citizens, and there would be . . . priests, whose numbers varied according to the quality of the deceased; his body would be taken thence to the church in which he had wanted to be buried, being borne on the shoulders of his peers, amidst the funeral pomp of candles and dirges. But as the ferocity of the plague began to mount, this practice all but disappeared entirely. . . . Not only did people die without having many women about them but a great number departed this life without anyone at all to witness their going. Few indeed were those to whom the lamentations and bitter tears of their relatives were accorded; on the contrary, more often than not bereavement was the signal for laughter and witticisms and general jollification."

The living hurriedly bury the dead in large pits. With thousands dying, the living had little opportunity for the ceremony that usually accompanied death.

The Plague Sweeps North

Heavily urbanized northern and central Italy had already suffered serious calamities in the five years before the arrival of the Black Death, and the area was in a near-crisis state when the Black Death struck. Earthquakes had severely damaged a number of towns, including Rome, Pisa, and Venice. A six-month period of almost continuous rain had destroyed crops and caused flooding. Poor harvests of the 1340s caused food shortages, and the cost of food soared. Famine was a serious problem. In the spring of 1347, in the town of Orvieto, just north of Rome, the town council ordered that all the prisoners in jail be set free, "for if they remain they will die of hunger."[16] Elsewhere, records of the time say that "many people died of hunger and people ate grass and weeds as if they had been wheat."[17] The exhausted and malnourished people of Italy were ill equipped to meet their worst catastrophe yet, the Black Death.

The plague entered northern and central Italy at its great seaports. Most historians believe it reached Genoa in December 1347, although a Flemish chronicler gives a slightly different date along with a vivid description of its arrival:

In January of the year 1348, three galleys put in at Genoa, driven by a fierce wind from the East, horribly infected. . . . When the inhabitants of Genoa learnt this, and saw how suddenly and irremediably [the sailors] infected other people, they were driven forth

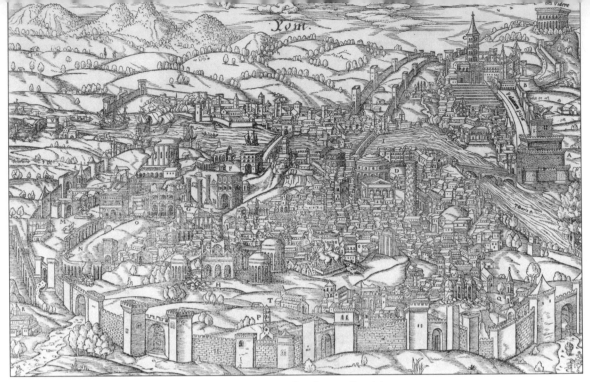

*The ancient city of Rome was especially heavily hit by the plague. Its citizens
had already been devastated by destructive earthquakes and poor harvests.*

from that port by burning arrows and divers engines of war; for no man dared touch them; nor was any man able to trade with them, for if he did, he would be sure to die forthwith. Thus they were scattered from port to port.[18]

When the plague-infested ships sailed into the port of Genoa, that city's population was about 100,000. Within a few months, the Black Death had killed 30,000 to 40,000 citizens of the town.

Plague arrived at the port city of Pisa in January 1348, and traveled inland along the roads of commerce to the rich and populous region of Italy known as Tuscany. By April the Black Death had reached the major inland cities of Italy. Throughout Tuscany, towns that had already suffered through famines faced even more suffering. Pistoia was an important and prosperous market town of about twenty-four thousand when the plague struck in May 1348. Pistoian authorities tried to quarantine the town, refusing to allow visitors or imported goods to enter. Their efforts were useless. More than nine thousand inhabitants died.

Siena, just thirty miles south of Florence, was one of Europe's most important banking centers. When the Black Death struck in May 1348, the town was busy building a new cathedral. More than half the townspeople died of plague, and the project was abandoned. So many workers and master masons were lost, and the grief of the survivors was so great, that they could not carry on. The unfinished cathedral stands to this day, a witness to the visitation of the Black Death.

The End of the World

The Black Death struck so many so quickly, and their death was so horrible, that people's fear of contagion left them numb to every other human feeling. In his Chronicle of Siena, *quoted in Robert Gottfried's* The Black Death, *Agnolo di Tura described what happened when the plague struck Siena.*

"The mortality in Siena began in May. It was a cruel and horrible thing. . . . Indeed, one who did not see such horribleness can be called blessed. And the victims died almost immediately. They would swell beneath the armpits and in their groins, and fall over while talking. Father abandoned child, wife husband, one brother another; for this illness seemed to strike through breath and sight. And so they died. And none could be found to bury the dead for money or friendship. Members of a household brought their dead to a ditch as best they could, without priest, without divine offices. Nor did the death bell sound. And in many places in Siena great pits were dug and piled deep with the multitude of dead. And they died by the hundreds, both day and night, and all were thrown in those ditches and covered with earth. And as soon as those ditches were filled, more were dug. And I, Agnolo di Tura, called the Fat, buried my five children with my own hands, and so did many others likewise. And so many died that all believed it was the end of the world."

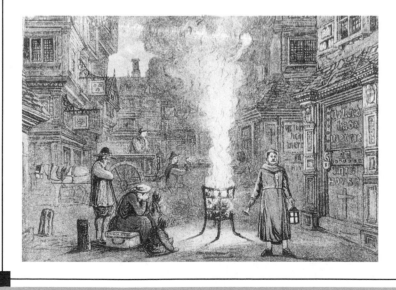

A monk helps gather the corpses of plague victims along a medieval street.

Venice tried to contain the plague by quarantining ships for forty days. But the Venetians did not realize that while the ships sat in port, flea-infested rats carried the plague to shore.

The prosperous city of Venice tried all methods known at the time to contain disease. It already had a well-established sanitation and public health system, which included city physicians and hospitals. City officials developed a sophisticated quarantine system to hold the plague at bay. Bodies of plague victims were ferried on barges to islands in the lagoon, where they were buried at least five feet deep. Incoming ships were quarantined for forty days, and quarantine violators were condemned to death. As in other cities, many doctors fled Venice in terror and city officials allowed surgeons (who formerly were considered craftsmen) to take over for the absent physicians. All efforts failed. Within the eighteen months following December 1347, approximately 60 percent of Venetians perished.

Of all the important cities and towns throughout Italy, only Milan was relatively unscathed. The ruler of Milan was Archbishop Giovanni Visconti, head of the Visconti family, one of the most ruthless ruling families of the fourteenth century.

He was a despot, with absolute power. On his orders, the first three houses in the city that were struck with plague were completely walled up, leaving both the sick and the well inside to perish. This extreme action may have been responsible for Milan's comparatively low death rate—only 15 percent of its population died. The rest of Italy was not so fortunate.

Italy paid a high price for its dominance as the commercial center of Europe. Its many ports of entry were open doors that allowed different strains of the plague to enter the country from many sources, thus increasing the deadliness of the epidemic.

By the end of 1348—a little over a year from when it first reached Sicily—the Black Death had nearly run its course in Italy. The plague had taken a terrible toll in lives. Many scholars believe that overall between 40 and 50 percent of the total population of Italy perished in the Black Death.

In the meantime, the plague was spreading terror throughout the rest of Europe.

Chapter

3 The Black Death Sweeps Europe

"In A.D. 1348, the people of France and of almost the whole world were struck by a blow other than war."[19] So begins the chronicle of the French friar Jean de Venette for the year 1348. This blow was the Black Death, "pestilence and its attendant tribulations" as Friar Jean called it. The Black Death had first entered Europe through Italy, and from there it swept through Europe, carried by the black rats that infested every medieval merchant ship. The plague moved as quickly as men could travel, riding the ships that sailed the Mediterranean coast, westward to Spain, and up the navigable rivers to inland towns.

In January 1348, the Black Death reached Marseilles, France's principal seaport on the Mediterranean. By summer most of southern France was infected, including the city of Paris. The disease followed established trade routes; from Paris it swept north and west to England and east to Germany. It struck London in

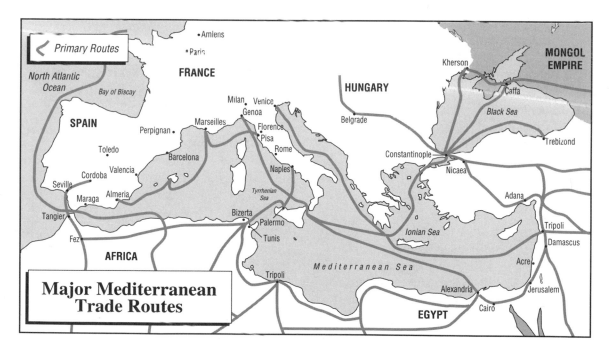

Major Mediterranean Trade Routes

THE BLACK DEATH SWEEPS EUROPE ■ 41

A Star over Paris

Jean de Venette, a Carmelite friar and a master of theology at the University of Paris, was a witness to a celestial phenomenon, which he believed was an omen of the plague. He writes of it in his Chronicle.

"In the month of August, 1348, after Vespers when the sun was beginning to set, a big and very bright star appeared above Paris, toward the west. It did not seem as stars usually do, to be very high above our hemisphere but rather very near. As the sun set and night came on, this star did not seem to me or to many other friars who were watching it to move from one place. At length, when night had come, this big star, to the amazement of all of us who were watching, broke into many different rays and, as it shed these rays over Paris toward the east, totally disappeared and was completely annihilated. Whether it was a comet or not . . . I leave to the decision of astronomers. It is, however, possible that it was a presage of the amazing pestilence to come."

September 1348, and by the end of 1349 it had completely engulfed England, Scotland, and Ireland; by 1350 it had completed its journey through Germany, Denmark, Sweden, Holland, and Finland. The Black Death ran its course by the end of 1351, ironically coming full circle to the Russian steppe of central Asia, from where it had first started its deadly journey.

Although it took four years for the plague to make its way through Europe, in most rural areas it completed its kill in about four to six months, then disappeared. In the crowded cities, with their dense population and lack of sanitation, the plague sometimes disappeared over the winter and then started up again in the spring to kill for another few months. Not only the large numbers of dead but also the speed with which the plague depleted the population—killing one-third to one-half of the people in a few months—left the survivors reeling in shock and despair.

The Plague in Villages and Countryside

By 1348 peasants who worked the lands of southern France were in a demoralized state brought on by the beginnings of the Hundred Years' War and the continued looting of their possessions. Both the French and English armies destroyed the peasants' crops and fields. Many of these poor people believed that the plague was a final blow sent by God to utterly destroy them.

Overall the southern provinces of France suffered about a 50 percent death rate. In some selected districts, however, mortality was as high as 70 percent. As one might imagine, when half of a community's population dies in a short time, not enough hands are left to work the fields and not enough people are left to purchase the goods produced. For example, the province of Languedoc had specialized in the cultivation of grapes, a cash crop. The Black Death caused a severe drop in demand, and the region did not even begin to recover until the sixteenth century.

The tide of death continued spreading, moving up river valleys and from village to village, arriving in the region of Normandy in France by July 1348. Black flags flew from village church steeples to warn of the Black Death. In the town of Ste. Marie, half the population died by September. As was the case everywhere else, so many died so quickly that survivors could not keep up with burials. As one observer records, "bodies of the dead decayed in putrefaction on the pallets where they had breathed their last."[20] The plague killed about 30 percent of the population of Normandy.

The plague reached out to every corner of France. No one, of high or low birth, was exempt. In the region of Bordeaux it killed Princess Joan, the daughter of King Edward III of England, who was traveling to Castile to marry the son of the king.

As it traveled northward, the Black Death laid waste to the countryside. According to the chronicles of Gilles Li Muisis:

It is almost impossible to [believe] the mortality throughout the whole country. Travelers, merchants, pilgrims and others who have passed through it declare that they have found cattle wandering without herdsmen in the fields, towns and waste-lands; that they have seen barns and wine-cellars standing wide open, houses empty and few people to be found anywhere. . . . And in many different areas, both lands and fields are lying uncultivated.[21]

The French town of Tournai on the border of the Netherlands was the home of the chronicler Gilles Li Muisis who describes what happened when the plague arrived:

An allegorical representation portrays the plague as a demon.

Every day the bodies of the dead were borne to the churches, now five, now ten, now fifteen, and in the parish of St. Brice, sometimes twenty or thirty. In all parish churches the curates, parish clerks and sextons, to get their fees, rang morning, evening, and night the passing bells, and by this the whole population of the city, men and women alike, began to be filled with fear.[22]

In normal times, Tournai's church bells were tolled to signal a funeral taking place. But so many people died so quickly, the bells seemed to toll constantly, a continual reminder to the townspeople of their great losses and their own impending death. To alleviate public fear and despair, the authorities quickly forbade the tolling of death bells and limited funeral attendance to two mourners. Tournai's authorities went one step further in hope of stemming the plague by raising the town's moral standards: They prohibited cursing, gambling, and working on Sundays and ordered all unmarried couples who were living together either to marry or to live apart. The prohibition against gambling caused the local manufacturer of dice to begin making prayer beads instead. Although the town's morality may have benefited, the plague went unchecked.

The Black Death reached southern England in late summer 1348 and swept northward through the following year. The Scots rejoiced to see their old enemy, England, staggering under the assault of the Black Death, and in the summer of 1349, anxious to take advantage of England's troubles, the Scots raised an army for invasion. But the army never crossed the border. By July, the plague had reached Scotland, killing much of the army and demoralizing the rest. The chronicler John of Fordun describes the plague's ravages:

> There was in the kingdom of Scotland so great a pestilence and plague

Surprised by Sudden Death

The Black Death entered England through its many ports. Chronicler Henry Knighton, a canon from a parish in Leicester, gives this account of the plague's arrival in Gottfried's The Black Death.

"Then the dreadful pestilence made its way along the coast by Southampton and reached Bristol, where almost the whole strength of the town perished, as it was surprised by sudden death; for few kept their beds more than two or three days, or even half a day. Then this cruel death spread on all sides, following the course of the sun. And there died at Leicester, in the small parish of Holy Cross, 400; in the parish of St. Margaret's, Leicester, 700; and so in every parish, in a great multitude."

England was struck by plague in 1348. The Scots enjoyed watching their English enemies die from the disease until they, too, began to die in droves.

among men . . . as, from the beginning of the world even unto modern times, had never been heard of by men. . . . For to such a pitch did the plague wreak its cruel spite that nearly a third of mankind were thereby made to pay the debt of nature. Moreover, by God's will, this evil led to a strange and unwonted kind of death, insomuch that the flesh of the sick was sometimes puffed out and swollen, and they dragged out their earthly life for barely two days.[23]

The Black Death reached Scandinavia in 1349. As the story goes, an English merchant ship carrying a cargo of wool set sail from England bound for the port of Bergen in Norway. When the ship neared Bergen, it ran aground and Norwegian officials boarded it to investigate. To their horror, the entire crew lay dead, having been stricken with plague during the voyage. The story may or may not be true, but it remains that Scandinavia would certainly have been infected by plague from some other source.

As the town of Bergen quickly became infected, leading citizens fled to the mountains to build a secluded community where they hoped to be safe from the disease. But the plague followed. All but one member of the new community died—a little girl. Somehow the child survived and was discovered years later. She had become like a wild animal, and she feared human beings. Her rescuers named her Rype, which means "wild bird." Eventually she re-entered society, grew up, and married. As sole survivor of the community, she and her heirs inherited all the property originally claimed by the community. For several centuries afterward, the Rype family was an important landowner in the area.

To the west of Scandinavia lay the most distant settlement of Christian Europe—Greenland. During the comparatively warm climate of the twelfth century, small fishing and hunting settlements had been established by the Scandinavians and Icelanders. These settlements depended on Scandinavia for provisions, and the periodic visitors from Europe brought the plague to Greenland. As Scandinavians became preoccupied by their own trials, they abandoned their commerce with Greenland. When Norwegian sailors finally returned to Greenland in the fifteenth century, they reported seeing only wild cattle and deserted villages.

The plague continued its relentless sweep across Europe. As early as June 1348, the plague had crossed the Alps and entered Bavaria. The *Neuburg Chronicles* record that in Styria, a region in the Austrian Alps,

> Men and women, driven to despair, wandered around as if mad . . . cattle were left to stray unattended in the fields for no one had any inclination to concern themselves about the future. The wolves, which came down from the mountains to attack the sheep, acted in a way which had never been heard of before. As if alarmed by some invisible warning they turned and fled back into the wilderness.[24]

The Plague on Manors and in Monasteries

In England, meticulous manorial records were kept, and historians have learned much about the lives of medieval people by examining these records of the daily affairs of manors. Throughout the prosperous English West Midlands, the fertile wheat-producing region, manor records indicate that the high death rates caused severe labor shortages. According to chronicler Henry Knighton of Leicester, "So few servants and laborers were left that no one knew where to turn for help."[25] The plague struck the managers of the manorial estates as well. The manager of Cuxham Manor in Oxford had held his post from 1311 until his death from the plague in March 1349. His appointed successor died in April 1349, a third appointed manager died in June, and a fourth in July. Eventually, the manor lands were leased out.

Not only workers and managers of English estates were taken by the Black

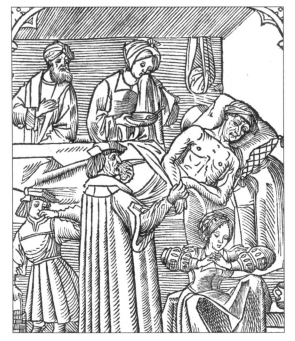

A doctor visits a plague victim. Often, a medieval doctor's remedies, which included bleeding the victim, further weakened patients and contributed to their death.

Death—livestock died as well. The most alarming losses were the great numbers of sheep that died throughout the country. Henry Knighton reports that more than five thousand sheep died in just one field, "their bodies so corrupted by the plague that neither bird nor beast would touch them."[26] Wool was one of England's most important exports, and the loss of so many sheep was an enormous hardship.

At the monastery and manor of St. Albans, chronicler William of Deves left his account of the first person to die from the plague, the Abbot Michael of Mentmore:

> The Abbot was the first to suffer from the dread disease, which was later to carry off his monks. He began to feel the first symptoms on Maundy Thursday [the Thursday before Easter Sunday], but out of reverence for the festival and remembering our Lord's humility, he celebrated High Mass. . . . The next day, when his sickness became worse, he took to his bed and, as a true Catholic, made his confession with a contrite heart. . . . Amidst the sorrow of all who surrounded him, he endured until noon on Easter Sunday.[27]

Following the abbot's death, forty-seven monks died in a matter of weeks, including the new abbot, and the monastery was abandoned.

Because people in monasteries lived so close together, when one person became infected by the plague, others soon fell victim as well. The Italian poet Petrarch's brother Gherardo was a Carthusian monk and the last survivor of his monastery. After burying thirty-four of his fellow monks in just a few weeks, he was left alone with only the company of a pet dog. He fled, leaving death and the deserted monastery behind.

In a procession, monks carry holy images before an emperor. In spite of their ascetic lifestyle, monks were also heavily afflicted by the plague.

At the monastery of the Minorite Friars in Kilkenny, Ireland, Brother John Clyn, one of the humblest clergy in Ireland, was the last survivor among the brothers. He faithfully recorded the events of the plague and concluded his record with the following comment:

> I, as if among the dead, waiting till death do come, have put into writing truthfully what I have heard and verified. And that the writing may not perish with the scribe and the work fail with the laborer, I add parchment to continue it, if by chance anyone may be left in the future, and any child of Adam may escape this pestilence and continue the work thus commenced.[28]

The Crowded Middle Ages

Crowded living in both city and country undoubtedly contributed to the rapid spread of the plague. Writer Philip Ziegler describes the lack of privacy in the Middle Ages in his book The Black Death.

"Privacy was not a concept close to the heart of medieval man and even in the grandest castle life was conducted in a perpetual crowd. Occleve [a medieval chronicler] writes of an earl and countess, their daughter and their daughter's governess who all slept in the same room. It would not be in the least surprising to know that they slept in the same bed as well if, indeed, there was a bed. In the houses of the poor, where the beds were an unheard-of luxury, it would not have been exceptional to find a dozen people sleeping on the floor of the same room. In the country villages, indeed in many urban houses as well, pigs and chickens and perhaps even ponies, cows and sheep, would share the common residence. Even if people had realized that such a step was desirable it would have been physically impossible to isolate the sick. The surprise is not how many households were totally wiped out but, rather, in how many cases some at least of the inhabitants survived."

A drawing depicts a typical overcrowded medieval town. The close quarters and lack of sanitation provided a perfect breeding ground for the plague.

On the parchment provided by Brother John, another handwriting informs the reader that Brother John did indeed die of plague.

Throughout the European countryside, on manors, in monasteries, and in small villages, the Black Death destroyed large numbers of the population. When the survivors—if there were any—left to find another community to join or to migrate to the cities, the villages disappeared, taken back by the wilderness, leaving scarcely a grassy mound to remind passers-by where a vital human community had once been.

In some areas, abandonment of villages was deliberate. As populations declined, landholders were unable to keep remaining agricultural workers or unable to pay the increased wages demanded by them. Consequently, the landowners stopped cultivating marginal lands, especially those that had been *assarts* in the twelfth and thirteenth centuries. While the richest farmland was kept under cultivation, marginal lands were turned to pasture or allowed to return to their natural state. This abandonment of rural areas, common across Europe, was called *Wustungen*. More than thirteen hundred villages in England alone were abandoned between 1350 and 1500.

The Crisis of Cities and Towns

Paris was one of the great cities of Europe, with a population of somewhere between 80,000 and 200,000 when the Black Death arrived in May or June of 1348. Paris was the home of a renowned university and a medical school and boasted more doctors than any other city in Europe. However, neither doctors nor priests could stem the tide of the Black Death.

The plague seemed mild at first, compared to other areas. But it gradually grew in ferocity until it peaked in November and December, when as many as eight hundred people died each day. The plague continued to torment Parisians until the winter of 1349 when it finally disappeared.

As in other areas, many doctors and clergy who should have been tending the sick fled in fear. Friar Jean de Venette records a notable exception:

> So high was the mortality at the Hotel-Dieu [a hospital] in Paris that for a long time, more than five hundred dead were carried daily with great devotion in carts to the cemetery of the Holy Innocents in Paris for burial. A very great number of the saintly sisters of the Hotel-Dieu who, not fearing to die, nursed the sick in all sweetness and humility . . . a number too often renewed by death, rest in peace with Christ, as we may piously believe.[29]

By the time the Black Death had run its course, about one-third of the population of Paris had died. In rural areas of France and throughout Europe, populations sometimes took centuries to recover. However, Paris was a brilliant cosmopolitan center, and like other great cities of Europe, as soon as the plague epidemic passed, the city swelled again with immigrants attracted to its many economic and cultural opportunities.

The city of London was struck in September 1348. Despite improvements in its sanitation system, London was still a filthy, crowded city, whose poor, often undernourished inhabitants were vulnerable targets for germs of all kinds. City officials attempted to enforce health and sanitation measures and keep out visitors, but the plague could not be stopped. It arrived in the fall, stayed throughout the winter, and grew ever more deadly as spring turned to summer. In a two-month period in the spring of 1349, 2,000 people were buried in one cemetery alone—more than 33 on an average day. But that was only the beginning. By summer 1349, records indicate an average of 290 people died daily. When Parliament was due to convene at Westminster, just outside the city walls, King Edward III delayed it, later giving as his reason

> the plague of deadly pestilence [that] had suddenly broken out in the said place and the neighbourhood, and daily increased in severity so that grave fears were entertained for the safety of those coming there at that time.[30]

The plague lingered in London well into 1350, killing 35 to 40 percent of the population. But, as happened in Paris, once the plague passed people flocked to London, attracted by the excitement and economic opportunity of urban life.

Across Europe, cities struck by the plague suffered the same problems. The common business of everyday life broke down. Chronicler Michael of Piazza reports that "Magistrates and notaries refused to come and make the wills of the dying . . . even the priests did not come to hear confessions."[31] Everywhere the Black Death struck, frightened clergy refused to attend the dying, often fleeing their parishes completely. Frightened doctors refused to treat the sick, and many fled to the countryside. Guy de Chauliac, physician to the pope, claims the only reason he did not flee his post, even though he was in constant fear, was because he wanted "to avoid infamy."

A ward in the Hotel-Dieu, a hospital in Paris, where as many as five hundred people died of the plague each day.

People sing and dance in defiance of the plague. Since adhering to God's rules did not seem to help deter the plague, people turned to pleasure to enjoy the limited time they had left.

The death of so many governing officials from large cities to small villages caused a crisis in government, as historian Barbara Tuchman explains:

> In Siena [Italy] four of the nine members of the governing oligarchy died, in France one third of the royal notaries, in Bristol [England] 15 out of the 52 members of the Town Council or almost one third. Tax-collecting obviously suffered, with the result that Philip VI [of France] was unable to collect more than a fraction of the subsidy granted him by the Estates in the winter of 1347–48.[32]

The loss of common laborers contributed to the general chaos. Shops closed, and craft guilds had to shorten the lengths of their apprenticeships so that new craftsmen could be quickly trained to fill the vacancies. Some guilds had to lower their quality standards, since so many experienced craftsmen were lost and the general level of skills had fallen. Construction was halted—often never to be resumed—for lack of skilled labor. So many street cleaners and carters died that cities became choked with garbage and filth, adding to the unhealthy conditions. In 1349 King Edward of England wrote to the mayor of London complaining that city streets were "foul with human feces and the air of the city poisoned to the great danger of men passing, especially in this time of infectious disease."[33]

People were so shocked and dazed they could not carry on the routines of daily life. Chroniclers routinely report that most people believed that they themselves

Abandoning Hope

Plague devastated the countryside, where many people simply dropped dead by the road. Those who were left lost hope for the future, believing they too would soon be dead. In his book The Decameron, *Giovanni Boccaccio describes the scene in the Italian countryside.*

"In the scattered hamlets and countryside proper, the poor unfortunate peasants and their families had no physicians or servants whatever to assist them, and collapsed by the wayside, in their fields, and in their cottages at all hours of the day and night, dying more like animals than human beings. . . . They . . . grew apathetic in their ways, disregarded their affairs, and neglected their possessions. Moreover they all behaved as though each day was to be their last, and far from making provision for the future by tilling their lands, tending their flocks, and adding to their previous labours, they tried in every way they could think of to squander the assets already in their possession. Thus it came about that oxen, asses, sheep, goats, pigs, chickens, and even dogs (for all their deep fidelity to man) were driven away and allowed to roam freely through the fields, where the crops lay abandoned and had not even been reaped, let alone gathered in."

would soon be dead, and so they showed little hope or concern for the future. People squandered their money, adopting an attitude of "eat, drink, and be merry, for tomorrow you may die," as Boccaccio describes:

> People behaved as though their days were numbered, and treated their belongings and their own persons with equal abandon. Hence most houses had become common property, and any passing stranger could make himself at home as naturally as though he were the rightful owner.[34]

Law and order broke down throughout Europe. Bands of thieves and cutthroats roamed the countryside. The cities were equally lawless, and robbers freely looted the houses left empty by the Black Death.

In Paris, as in other cities, the wealthy fled, the poor looted and drank away their fear, and only the gravediggers traveled through the city. It seemed to many decent citizens that Paris was near a state of anarchy, and that it was, if not the end of the world, the end of civilized society.

The Pope and Clergy

When the Black Death struck in 1348, Avignon, France, was the home of Pope Clement VI. The papacy had been moved from Rome to Avignon in 1309, where it remained until 1377. As the papal residence, Avignon was a wealthy and crowded city, filled with clergy of all rank, bustling with the comings and goings of visitors on church business. Being a high official of the church was no protection from the plague, however: Nine cardinals (one-third the total number) and seventy lesser church officials died. In all, about half the total population of Avignon was lost. It was reported that seven thousand houses were empty because all their inhabitants had died.

The pope himself was spared. Guy de Chauliac, physician to the pope, insisted that he sit alone in his chambers between two huge fires of aromatic wood. The pope followed his physician's advice and escaped infection. However, it was more likely that since it was August, the fleas were discouraged by the heat of the fires. Furthermore, the pope left the city when the plague was at its worst.

Pope Clement VI did what he could to address the crisis of the Black Death across Europe. He granted special permission for laypeople to hear the last confession of a dying person when no priest was available. He also ordered prayers and processions through the streets to ask God and the saints to save the world from the terrible pestilence. The processions quickly grew enormous, attracting people from all over the region. According to one chronicle, some processions drew as many as two thousand people.

> Many of both sexes were barefooted, some were in sack cloth, some covered with ashes, wailing as they walked, tearing their hair, and lashing themselves with scourges even to the point where blood was drawn.[35]

The pope soon realized that these processions were a breeding ground for mass hysteria, and he abruptly forbade them.

While the pope took his duties seriously, many other clergy did not. Throughout Europe, just when spiritual comfort and reassurance were needed most, many clergy deserted their posts and left their parishioners to face the Black Death alone. Worse, some of those who did stay charged outrageous fees for their services. In general, though, members of the clergy ministered selflessly to their parishioners, and because of their service were even more likely than their parishioners to die. Records of mortality throughout England show that priests had a higher rate of mortality than the people they served. In all, England suffered the loss of nearly half its clergy. In Germany as well, the death rate for clergy was higher than for the lay populace. Nevertheless,

To respond to the lack of clergy and a need for people to still participate in religious ritual, Pope Clement VI altered some church practices.

what people remembered most were not the sacrifices, but the failures. The church was being criticized for its worldliness long before the Black Death arrived, and despite the many dedicated and pious clergy members who died caring for their charges, the common perception was that the clergy in general neglected its duty.

Many clergy members who escaped the plague grew wealthy in the years after the Black Death. Many dying people willed their worldly goods to the local parishes and monasteries, hoping to win salvation with their generous bequests.

A devoted priest administers the last rites to a man dying of the plague. Their close contact with plague victims made members of the clergy especially susceptible to contracting it.

However, while many parishes and monasteries prospered, many others were barely able to maintain themselves because of the loss of people who supported them. The poorer parishes were scorned by many surviving clergy, who grew more greedy and sought positions in richer parishes, which guaranteed them a better income. The fourteenth-century English poet William Langland complained about the priests' love of silver:

> Parsons and parish priests complained to the Bishop
> That their parishes were poor since the pestilence time
> And asked leave and licence in London to dwell
> And sing requiems for stipends, for silver is sweet.[36]

A Horrible Loneliness—The End of the Black Death

The Black Death completed its deadly journey and died out by the end of 1351. This catastrophe was different from those to which the world was accustomed, such as earthquakes or floods, and it brought an unnatural response. The shock of losing one-third or one-half or three-fourths of their people in a few months was more than most communities could stand. Victims of the Black Death died a horrible death, suffering terrible agony and exuding a horrible stench; the disease spread in such a mysterious, almost supernatural way; and so very many died. The Black Death was so feared that normal social ties collapsed and the natural human responses that hold communities together failed. People did not reach out to those

The Plague's Toll

When the Black Death had run its course, it left Europe devastated and depopulated. In his Chronicle, *quoted in Ziegler's* The Black Death, *Giovanni Villani of Florence summarized the Black Death's effects. Villani deliberately left the end of the last sentence blank. He had intended to fill in the date the plague finally passed, but he himself became one of its victims.*

"Having grown in vigor in Turkey and Greece and having spread thence over the whole Levant and Mesopotamia and Syria and Chaldea and Cyprus and Rhodes and all the islands of the Grcek archipelago, the said pestilence leaped to Sicily, Sardinia and Corsica and Elba, and from there soon reached all the shores of the mainland. And of eight Genoese galleys which had gone to the Black Sea only four returned, full of infected sailors, who were smitten one after the other on the return journey. And all who arrived at Genoa died, and they corrupted the air to such an extent that whoever came near the bodies died shortly thereafter. And it was a disease in which there appeared certain swellings in the groin and under the armpit, and the victims spat blood, and in three days they were dead. And the priest who confessed the sick and those who nursed them so generally caught the infection that the victims were abandoned and deprived of confession, sacrament and medicine, and nursing. . . . And many lands and cities were made desolate. And the plague lasted until_____ "

in need; on the contrary, they avoided them, even abandoning their own families. Chroniclers all across Europe reported the breakdown of family bonds. According to Guy de Chauliac, "A father did not visit his son, nor the son his father. Charity was dead."[37]

Chroniclers throughout Europe often claimed death rates higher than the original population, but they cannot be blamed for exaggerating the numbers of dead. They were not trying to deliberately mislead: The numbers of dead were so overwhelming that to the observers it may have seemed as though nearly the whole world was dying. They, like other survivors, were shocked, unable to comprehend the enormous losses. As the Italian poet Petrarch wrote:

Has one ever seen anything like this, ever heard reports of similar occurrence? In what annals has one ever read that the houses were empty, the cities deserted, the farms untended, the fields full of corpses, and that everywhere a horrible loneliness prevailed?[38]

Chapter

4 Potions, Penance, and Pogroms: The Search for Answers

An air of evil mystery surrounded the Black Death. People had no idea what caused it or how to combat it. Medieval medicine had no concept of microbes or of how infectious diseases spread. Inexplicably, some people were stricken with the plague while others escaped. To add to the mystery, the plague appeared in more than one form. The bubonic variety caused buboes under the arms and in the groin and neck and usually struck during warm weather, when fleas were active. In cold weather, however, when people were susceptible to colds and pneumonia, the disease sometimes took the pneumonic form. In such cases the microbes attacked the weakened lungs of people suffering from some respiratory ailment; from there it spread in much the same way the common cold is spread, from person to person, through coughing. Thus in its pneumonic form, the rat and flea intermediaries were bypassed. The pneumonic plague was much more deadly, killing 95 percent or more of its victims in three days or less, and infecting others so quickly that people believed it was spread simply by looking in the eye of an infected person.

Medieval people searched for answers, but as Giovanni Boccaccio observed, the plague remained a mystery:

Some say that it descended upon the human race through the influence of the heavenly bodies, others that it was a punishment signifying God's right-

Death as a reaper and mounted hunter randomly cuts down the citizenry.

God's Marvellous Remedy

Many people believed that the Black Death was God's punishment for sin. The English chronicler Henry Knighton expresses both this idea and the general medieval antiwoman attitude when he indignantly describes women who behaved in a way he considered sinful and unseemly. He considered the Black Death a "marvellous remedy" for their behavior. Knighton is quoted in G. G. Coulton's book Medieval Panorama.

"In those days, there arose a huge rumour and outcry among the people, because when tournaments were held, in almost every place, a band of women would come as if to share the sport, dressed in [men's clothing]—sometimes [as many as] 40 or 50 ladies, of the fairest and comeliest (though I say not, of the best) among the whole kingdom. Thither they came [dressed] in party-coloured tunics, one colour or pattern on the right side and another on the left, with short hoods that had pendants like ropes wound round their necks, and belts thickly studded with gold and silver—nay they even wore, in pouches slung across their bodies, those knives which are called "daggers" in the vulgar tongue; and thus they rode on choice war-horses or other splendid steeds to the place of tournament. There and thus they spent and lavished their possessions, and wearied their bodies with fooleries and wanton buffoonery. . . . But God, in this matter, as in all others, brought marvellous remedy. . . . That same year and the next came the general mortality throughout the world."

eous anger at our iniquitous way of life. . . . In the face of its onrush, all the wisdom and ingenuity of man were unavailing.[39]

Although people of medieval Europe did not know the direct cause of the plague, they believed without reservation that God was overseeing the world, judging human behavior, and ready to punish the wicked, and they concluded that this mysterious, evil Black Death was a punishment from an angry God. As one Italian writer exclaimed: "Tell, O Sicily, and ye, the many islands of the sea, the judgments of God! Confess, O Genoa, what thou has done, since we of Genoa and Venice are compelled to make God's chastisement manifest."[40] Fearful and bewildered people of the time attempted to make sense of this terrible catastrophe.

Science and the Black Death

In the fourteenth century, astrology was widely acknowledged as a science, although it was a strange combination of astronomical observations and magical

An Unbelievable Contagion

In The Decameron, *Giovanni Boccaccio describes how contagious the disease appeared to be.*

"It is a remarkable story that I have to relate. And were it not for the fact that I am one of many people who saw it with their own eyes, I would scarcely dare to believe it. . . . The plague . . . was of so contagious a nature that very often it visibly did more than simply pass from one person to another. In other words, whenever an animal other than a human being touched anything belonging to a person who had been stricken or exterminated by the disease, it not only caught the sickness, but died from it almost at once. To all of this, as I have just said, my own eyes bore witness on more than one occasion. One day, for instance, the rags of a pauper who had died from the disease were thrown into the street, where they attracted the attention of two pigs. . . . The pigs first of all gave the rags a thorough mauling with their snouts after which they took them between their teeth and shook them against their cheeks. And within a short time they began to writhe as though they had been poisoned, then they both dropped dead to the ground, spreadeagled upon the rags that had brought about their undoing."

thinking that claimed human physiology was subject to the planets. Theories of astrology were accepted even by the most learned doctors.

When the plague struck, the University of Paris boasted one of the most prestigious medical schools in Europe. King Philip VI of France asked the medical faculty of the university to explain the plague. After careful consideration, they announced that the plague was initially caused by a conjunction of the planets Saturn, Jupiter, and Mars in the sign of Aquarius that took place on March 20, 1345. This opinion became the official

"scientific" explanation but did not preclude the notion of God's punishment. Many people believed that the movement of planets was the method by which God's will was manifested on earth.

Other theories stressed the environmental rather than astrological causes for the plague. The most common theory was that the plague came from the East by some form of poisonous air. Reports had reached Europe of the many catastrophes in Asia—floods, famines, and cataclysmic earthquakes, all of which were real enough. Other reports were more fancy than fact—strange storms in which sheets of fire burned entire cities creating foul blasts of air that carried the infection to Europe. Others theorized that the earthquakes released poisonous gases into the air. The poisoned air supposedly drifted over Europe, bringing pestilence to everything in its path. Indeed, the Black Death did seem to drift across the continent like a cloud drifting in the wind. Some physicians believed the plague was contained in clouds of warm air from the south, and they advised closing up windows with southern exposure.

In some cases, both the astrological and the environmental theories combined. According to a physician at the University of Padua in Italy, planetary influences caused

> poisonous material which is generated about the heart and the lungs. . . . Through properties of poisonous va-

pors having been communicated by means of air breathed in and out, great extension and [movement] of this plague takes place, not only from man to man but from country to country.[41]

The answer to why some people were stricken and others escaped the disease rested on the idea of humors, the fundamental basis of medical theory in the Middle Ages. According to this theory, the human body had four humors: yellow bile, which was hot and dry; black bile, which was cold and dry; blood, which was hot and moist; and phlegm, which was cold and moist. The four humors of the human body corresponded to the four elements in the world: fire, earth, air, and water. If the humors in the body were in balance, then the person was healthy. An imbalance in the humors caused disease, and the physician attempted to restore the

Panels depict two of the four humors, melancholic (left) and sanguine (right). Medieval doctors believed that those with "warmer" temperaments were more likely to fall victim to the plague.

balance. An individual's temperament was determined by the predominance of one or more of the humors.

Most physicians believed that individuals with a temperament governed by the hot and moist were more susceptible to the plague. They thought that women were more vulnerable, and if they were young, athletic, and sensual, they were even more susceptible to the plague. Of course, no records exist to prove whether a high percentage of young and athletic females fell to the plague. The notion of the vulnerability of women may have reflected the general antifeminist attitudes of the church during the Middle Ages.

In parts of northern Europe, plague was thought to originate from a Pest Maiden who emerged as a blue flame from the mouth of a dead victim and flew to the next house to infect it. According to Lithuanian legend, the Pest Maiden waved a red scarf through an open door or window to bring the plague. One story tells of a brave peasant who chopped off the hand of the Pest Maiden as she waved the red scarf in the door. The peasant was stricken and died for his deed, but his village was spared the plague. The red scarf was thereafter preserved in the village church.

Fighting the Black Death

Medieval doctors could not prevent the plague any more than they could explain it. Nevertheless, they tried. People were advised to avoid marshy and low-lying areas where poisonous air might settle, and coastal areas where the poisonous air could drift in from the sea. Physicians throughout Europe believed that the

A medieval doctor diagnoses a patient, determining that the bubo on his arm is a sign of the plague.

plague was most dangerous in cities, and they urged people where possible to flee to the countryside. In fact, the cities were more plague-ridden than the rural areas in Italy and southern France, but in northern Europe the disease struck most heavily in the sparsely populated rural areas. The major textile manufacturing towns of Bruges, Ypres, Brussels, Ghent, and Antwerp had populations of twenty thousand to sixty thousand. Surprisingly, their death rate was 20 to 25 percent, much lower than adjacent rural areas, where death rates climbed to 30 to 35 percent.

Doctors also recommended that people remain secluded and avoid contact with others. Some physicians advised the procedure of phlebotomy, or therapeutic bleeding, to maintain a balance of the humors and to prepare the body to resist the plague. Purging with laxatives was another recommendation. Doctors also urged people to purify the "corrupted" air by burning fragrant woods, such as pine, juniper, or ash. People filled their homes with sweet-smelling flowers, aloe, amber, and herbs such as rosemary, whose good smells supposedly repelled the plague fumes. Bathing was discouraged because it opened pores and made the skin more susceptible to plague fumes. However, people were told to bathe their hands and feet with vinegar and rose water. If people had to leave their houses, they were advised to carry packets of sweet herbs to hold to their noses to keep away the noxious air. All this advice did little to discourage the plague, but it no doubt made normally smelly medieval dwellings more pleasant.

Diet was believed to be another important factor in warding off the plague. Moderation was important to keep a healthy balance of the humors. People were advised to avoid any food that spoiled readily, such as meat, fish, or dairy products. Doctors also suggested eating figs and nuts before breakfast. Later in the day spices such as myrrh, saffron, and pepper and vegetables such as onions, leeks, and garlic were to be taken to ward off the plague.

Doctors believed that sleep was important, but not too much of it and never during the day or after meals. Sleeping on the back was the worst possible position, since the poisonous air could descend through the nostrils to the lungs. The best way to sleep was to shift regularly from the right side to the left side to keep the liver's heat in balance.

Physicians also cautioned men against having intercourse with women, or even sleeping in a woman's bed. Again, this caution was no doubt a reflection of the medieval church's attitudes toward sin.

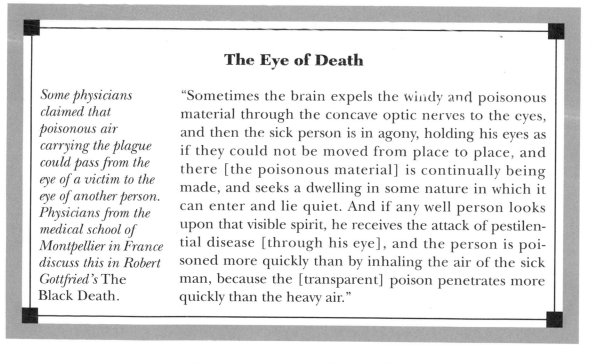

The Eye of Death

Some physicians claimed that poisonous air carrying the plague could pass from the eye of a victim to the eye of another person. Physicians from the medical school of Montpellier in France discuss this in Robert Gottfried's The Black Death.

"Sometimes the brain expels the windy and poisonous material through the concave optic nerves to the eyes, and then the sick person is in agony, holding his eyes as if they could not be moved from place to place, and there [the poisonous material] is continually being made, and seeks a dwelling in some nature in which it can enter and lie quiet. And if any well person looks upon that visible spirit, he receives the attack of pestilential disease [through his eye], and the person is poisoned more quickly than by inhaling the air of the sick man, because the [transparent] poison penetrates more quickly than the heavy air."

Warding Off This Appalling Evil

In The Decameron, *Giovanni Boccaccio describes the measures people of Florence took to avoid the plague.*

"Some people were of the opinion that a sober and abstemious mode of living considerably reduced the risk of infection. They therefore formed themselves into groups and lived in isolation from everyone else . . . consuming modest quantities of delicate foods and precious wines and avoiding all excesses. They refrained from speaking to outsiders, refused to receive news of the dead or the sick, and entertained themselves with music and whatever other amusements they were able to devise.

Others took the opposite view, and maintained that an infallible way of warding off this appalling evil was to drink heavily, enjoy life to the full, go round singing and merrymaking, gratify all of one's cravings whenever the opportunity offered, and shrug the whole thing off as one enormous joke. Moreover, they practised what they preached to the best of their ability, for they would visit one tavern after another, drinking all day and night to immoderate excess. . . .

There were many other people who steered a middle course . . . neither restricting their diet to the same degree as the first group, nor indulging so freely as the second in drinking and other forms of wantonness, but simply doing no more than satisfy their appetite. Instead of [locking themselves away], these people moved about freely, holding in their hands a posy of flowers, or fragrant herbs, or one of a wide range of spices, which they applied at frequent intervals to their nostrils, thinking it an excellent idea to fortify the brain with smells of that particular sort; for the stench of dead bodies, sickness, and medicines seemed to fill and pollute the whole of the atmosphere.

Some people, pursuing what was possibly the safer alternative, callously maintained that there was no better . . . remedy against a plague than to run away from it."

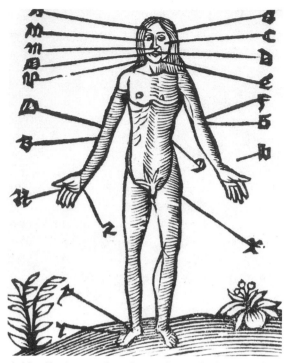

A bloodletting guide indicates from which veins blood should be drawn to release the poison in the blood and stop it from traveling to other parts of the body.

Treating the Plague

Once a person contracted the plague, the medical community could offer little practical help. Doctors were well aware of their helplessness, although few admitted it so bluntly as the Italian doctor Chalin de Vinario, who stated quite plainly that "Every pronounced case of plague is incurable."[42] Vinario knew that as a doctor he exposed himself to serious danger by treating plague patients, and like many doctors throughout Europe, he believed a doctor was entitled to an enormous fee if he chose to treat plague victims. Many doctors would not expose themselves for money or for honor, and they fled along with all others who were able to escape. Nevertheless, many doctors did remain faithful to their duty and treated plague victims, even though they knew that the treatment was probably doomed to fail.

Bleeding was the primary treatment. Doctors believed the blood vessels carried the disease throughout the body, and they used bleeding to remove the infection at the point where the buboes appeared. The physician John of Burgundy believed the body had natural emunctories, or passageways through which poison could be expelled from the body by bleeding. Various organs of the body had their own emunctories.

John explained the matter with scientific certainty:

> Thus, when the heart is attacked, we may be sure that the poison will fly to the emunctory of the heart, which is the armpit. But if it finds no outlet there it is driven to seek the liver, which again sends it to its own emunctory in the groin. If thwarted there, the poison will next seek the brain, when it will be driven either under the ears or to the throat.[43]

John believed that certain veins corresponded to these emunctories, and these veins could be bled to release the poison and stop its travels through the body, from heart to liver to brain.

Sometimes the buboes themselves were lanced or had curious remedies applied to them to draw the poison. The physician Gentile of Foligno favored applying a plaster made of the roots of white lilies, resin, and dried human feces to the buboes. Other physicians first lanced the buboes and then applied poultices made of violets. Another physician suggested killing an old rooster, cutting it through the back, and applying it to the buboes to draw the poison. The pope's physician, Guy de Chauliac, applied a poultice of figs mixed with cooked onions, yeast, and butter, and then lanced the buboes, a treatment he was convinced was effective. Apparently de Chauliac was able to cure himself by these means:

> Toward the end of the epidemic I fell ill with a continuous fever and a swelling in the groin and was ill for six weeks. I was in such danger that my companions believed that I would die, but the abscess became ripe, was treated as I have said, and I escaped by the grace of God.[44]

A doctor lances a bubo. After lancing the bubo, doctors applied poultices with a variety of ingredients, from human feces to violets.

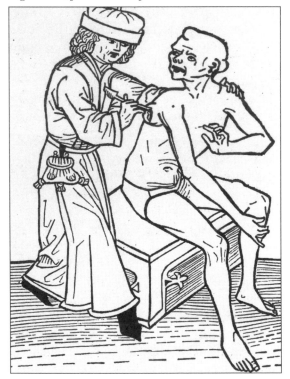

Other treatments included a variety of potions, pills, and compounds. Some were harmless and even soothing. One potion was made of apple syrup, peppermint, rose water, and lemon. Others were very expensive and often useless, such as expensive spices mixed with powdered pearls or powdered emeralds. These may have had psychological value, however, since many patients believed (as many believe today) that the more expensive the treatment, the more effective it must be. Gentile of Foligno recommended that patients drink a potion made of gold and quicksilver (mercury) mixed with water. Since mercury is highly toxic, if the patient did recover from the plague, he might very well have suffered the effects of mercury poisoning.

Prayers and Magic

The wealthy could afford expensive treatments and exotic potions, but common people had few resources for treatments. It mattered little, of course, for once the disease was contracted, the lord died as readily as the peasant, despite the expensive potions.

The first resource of the common people—and the wealthy—was prayer and penitence. Until they were banned by the pope, processions in which participants carried candles and relics of the saints through the streets of the city, praying to God and to the Virgin Mary for mercy, were popular. The town of Rouen in France attempted to appease the wrath of God by banning drinking, gambling, and swearing. Like every other measure desperate people tried, prayers, penance, and

A Medieval Recipe

Because the treatments prescribed by medieval physicians were so ineffective during the Black Death, people often brewed their own medicines, such as the following popular recipe taken from Gottfried's The Black Death.

"A medicine for the pestilence. Take five cups of rue [an aromatic medicinal plant] if it be a man, and if it be a woman leave out the rue, for rue is restorative to a man and wasting to a woman; and then take thereto five crops of tansey [a medicinal plant] and five little blades of columbine, and a great quantity of marigold flowers full of the small chives from the crops that are like saffron chives. And if you may not get the flowers, take the leaves, and then you must have of the marigolds more than the others. Then take an egg that is newly laid, and make a hole in either end, and blow out all that is within. And lay it to the fire and let it roast till it may be ground to powder, but do not burn it. Then take a quantity of good treacle [a compound used as antidote to poison] and bray [pound in] all these herbs therein with good ale, but do not strain them. And then make the sick drink it for three evenings and three mornings. If they [the sick] hold it, they shall have life."

A pharmacist mixes a potion for a patient. With no knowledge of the disease's spread or cause, doctors' remedies often caused more harm than good.

moral reform were useless in stemming the tide of the Black Death. As the poet William Langland wrote:

God is deaf now-a-days and deigneth not hear us,

And prayers have no power the Plague to stay.[45]

When prayers failed, the common people often turned to amulets, charms, and magical practices, which were sometimes not too different from the practice of the learned physicians. One remedy called for placing a live frog on the plague bubo. If the frog burst, the patient was

People pray in concert with a lay preacher in hopes of stemming the plague.

advised to place another frog on the sore until that frog burst and to continue the practice until all the poison was drawn. If the first frog did not burst, it was a sign that the patient would die.

The frightened and superstitious peasants grasped at anything they thought might save them from the plague. One popular remedy was using the word *abracadabra* as a magical charm to drive away sickness. The complete word was printed across the top of a piece of paper. Then, centered under the first line, the word was printed again, deleting the last letter, and then again, deleting the last letter, until the word dwindled away to form a triangle, as follows:

```
A B R A C A D A B R A
 A B R A C A D A B R
  A B R A C A D A B
   A B R A C A D A
    A B R A C A D
     A B R A C A
      A B R A C
       A B R A
        A B R
         A B
          A
```

The sick person hung the piece of paper around his or her neck. The magical prop-

erties of the word would supposedly cause the sickness to fade away, just as the word itself faded away.

The *abracadabra* charm was as ineffective a cure as bleeding, poultices of lily bulbs and human excrement, or potions of powdered pearls. Few patients who contracted bubonic plague survived; almost none who contracted pneumonic plague survived. In fact, mortality rates for the plague remained remarkably consistent for the next five hundred years. During an outbreak of plague early in the twentieth century, the death rate for bubonic plague was about 70 percent and for pneumonic plague almost 100 percent, despite the efforts of more sophisticated hospitals and medical care. The first effective treatment for plague was not developed until the 1940s, when antibiotics reduced the plague to no more of a threat than the common flu.

The Flagellants

People were desperate for some hope, some sign of mercy from an avenging God. The medical profession had failed utterly to protect them from the plague, or even to explain it. The church's failure was worse—not only were prayers and penances ineffective, the clergy often deserted their flock, leaving them to die without the comfort of a last confession and a final absolution of sins. Even before the plague struck, people were beginning to lose confidence in the church, with clergy members often speaking out against the institution, as one cleric did:

> How contemptible has the Church become! The pastors of the Church feed themselves instead of their flocks; the flocks they shear, or rather they flay them; they behave not like pastors but like wolves! All beauty has left the Church of God, from crown to heel there is no healthy spot on her![46]

The flagellant movement rose in 1348 in response to the failure of the church and the threat of the plague. The name *flagellant* refers to the members' practice of self-flagellation, or beating themselves with whips. Flagellants believed the sufferings they inflicted on themselves would atone for the sins of the world, appease an angry God, and bring an end to the plague. The flagellants emerged first in Hungary and spread throughout the Low Countries, Iberia, and parts of France. Known as the Brotherhood of the Flagellants or the Brethren of the Cross, the movement was most successful in Germany, especially in the German Rhineland. Penitents traveled in bands of two to three hundred, and sometimes up to one thousand, each under the control of a Master. Wearing long, hooded robes with red crosses emblazoned on the front, back, and hood, they marched from town to town.

When they arrived in a town, they gathered in front of the church or in the town square. Stripped to the waist and wearing only an ankle-length skirt, the flagellants began walking in a circle. One at a time, they threw themselves to the ground, face down with arms outstretched, in the form of a cross. Those that followed stepped over the out-

Flagellants believed that by beating themselves, they would take on the sin of the world and eliminate the plague.

The German Flagellants

As the flagellant movement was taken over by people who were interested mainly in power, the flagellants became increasingly antagonistic toward the church, as historian Norman Cohn points out in The Pursuit of the Millennium.

"The German flagellants in particular ended as uncompromising enemies of the Church who not only condemned the clergy but utterly [denied] the clergy's claim to supernatural authority. They denied that the sacrament of the Eucharist had any meaning; and when the host was elevated [by a priest during mass] they refused to show it reverence. They made a practice of interrupting church services, saying that their own ceremonies and hymns alone had value. They set themselves above pope and clergy, on the grounds that whereas [the Church had only] the Bible and tradition as the sources of their authority, they themselves had been taught directly by the Holy Spirit which had sent them out across the world. . . . They declared that any priest who contradicted them should be dragged from his pulpit and burnt at the stake. When two Dominicans [monks] ventured to dispute with a flagellant band they were stoned, one being killed and the other escaping only by flight. . . . At times flagellants would urge the populace to stone the clergy. . . . A French chronicler said that the flagellant movement aimed at utterly destroying the Church, taking over its wealth and killing all the clergy. There is no reason to think that [was an exaggeration]."

Flagellants lead a procession. The flagellants often expressed the anger and frustration against the church that many people felt in their helplessness against the plague.

stretched person, lightly striking him with a scourge. When all had fallen down, the group arose and began their flagellation. They used leather whips tipped with iron spikes to beat themselves upon the back as they sang hymns celebrating the Virgin Mary and the suffering of Jesus Christ. At certain points during the hymn, they would all fall down "as if struck by lightning." Lying on the ground with outstretched arms, they would sob and pray until the cue to arise and resume the flagellation. If at any time the circle was entered by a woman or by a priest, the ceremony was declared invalid by the Master and had to be repeated from the beginning. During the scourging, iron spikes often became embedded in the flesh and had to be torn free, causing much bleeding. The ceremony was performed twice each day and once in the evening, and the bodies of the flagellants became horribly swollen and bruised.

When the flagellants were recruited, they pledged to join the pilgrimage for 33½ days—in remembrance of the 33½ years that Jesus spent on earth—and to submit themselves to the discipline of the Master. They were forbidden to shave, to bathe, or even to change their clothes. They could wash their hands, but they had to kneel while doing so as a sign of humility. The most important restriction had to do with women—flagellants were ordered to avoid all contact with women, including their wives, even to the point of being forbidden to speak a word to a woman or being served at table by a woman. If they broke this rule, the Master beat them as they knelt before him, and then he commanded them to "Arise by the honor of pure martyrdom and henceforth guard yourself against sin!"[47]

Even though most clergy disapproved of the flagellants, the people of the towns and villages welcomed the penitent pilgrims, believing that the flagellants might save them from the plague. When news of an approaching flagellant procession reached a town, church bells were tolled, often over the objections of the parish priest, and residents went out to greet the travelers. The people were much affected by the ceremony, sobbing, moaning, and tearing their hair as the flagellants scourged themselves. Many believed the blood of the flagellants had special powers, and during the flagellation people collected the blood with cloths. During the flagellant visitations, local clergy usually wisely stayed out of sight.

The flagellant movement swept quickly across Europe, and though it was of short duration, it involved thousands of people. At a monastery in the Low Countries that was a stop for the pilgrim bands, twenty-five hundred flagellants passed through in a period of six months. At Tournai in northern France, a band arrived each week for a period of nearly two months. In his book *The Pursuit of the Millennium* author Norman Cohn explains how the flagellant hysteria swept across Europe:

To conceive the movement as a whole one must picture a number of regions passing one after another into a state of emotional agitation which would remain in full force for some three months and then gradually subside. In the East, where the movement began, it was over by the middle of the year [1349]. In central and southern Germany it began to wane soon after-

The flagellants became so heretical that the church banned the movement.

wards. In the Low Countries and northern France it lasted till late autumn.[48]

In the beginning, the flagellant movement attracted pious and respectable people—well-off merchants and even noblemen—who believed that their suffering might save people from the terrible plague. As the movement grew, abuses such as sexual misconduct crept in. Most respectable participants left the movement, leaving the fringe elements of society in charge. Many flagellants began claiming that their blood was equal to the blood of Jesus Christ. Some claimed that they had shared a meal with Jesus Christ or had spoken personally to the Virgin Mary. But the Black Death still raged on, and people were beginning to lose faith in the flagellants. The movement was taken over by people who were more interested in power than in penance, and they began to challenge the church. Finally Pope Clement banned the movement, threaten-

ing to excommunicate from the church any who took part in the flagellant processions. The pope's ban was the final blow. By 1350 the flagellants disappeared, as one chronicler describes, "vanishing as suddenly as they had come, like night phantoms or mocking ghosts."[49] Though successful at first in inspiring hope in the people, the flagellant movement had failed to stem the tide of the Black Death.

Pogroms

Drawing on a long history of anti-Semitism and inflamed by the flagellants, people turned on the Jews, claiming that they had brought the sickness by poisoning the wells.

The rights of Jews were severely restricted in medieval Europe—they were spurned as outsiders in a universally Christian society. They were labeled Christ-killers. They were accused of ritual blood sacrifices of Christian babies and any other monstrous deed the superstitious medieval imagination could conjure up. Barred from crafts and trades, they were tolerated primarily because they were moneylenders—one of the very few economic options open to them. In a Christian society whose kings and merchants were in constant need of ready cash, but which considered making money by lending money to be a sin called usury, the Jews proved useful. Nevertheless, they were always in a precarious position, ready scapegoats for a variety of society's misfortunes.

The Black Death was the greatest misfortune the medieval world experienced, and the Jews suffered accordingly. Jews died as readily as Christians, but still they were persecuted. The reason given was their supposed poisoning of wells. The rumors started when a Jewish physician, under the duress of medieval torture, confessed to being part of a conspiracy to poison wells. All across Europe, frightened and inflamed Christians turned their wrath on Jewish citizens.

The Jewish population in Iberia was the largest and most prosperous in the Mediterranean region. Jews had been treated better in Iberia than in any part of Christendom, holding many responsible positions in public service and in private businesses. The general breakdown of authority especially affected the Jews. Even though the royal authorities attempted to protect the Jews, Christians who were desperately searching for an explanation for their terrible scourge turned on them. The Black Death and the wrath of Christians nearly eliminated the prosperous Jewish communities of Iberia.

Jews suffered terribly in France, Germany, and Switzerland, as well, where the violence was often encouraged by flagellants. Thousands were massacred or burned alive; the lucky ones were driven out of the town. Most thinking people of the time dismissed the charges of well poisoning as ridiculous, pointing out that Jews drank the same water and died at the same rate as Christians. Physicians at the medical

A Jewish moneylender discusses terms with a client. Many people blamed the Jews for the plague.

schools in Paris and Montpellier flatly declared the charge to be false. Nevertheless, the anti-Semitic hysteria continued. Friar Jean de Venette chronicles the events:

> The Jews were suddenly and violently charged with infecting the wells and water, and corrupting the air. The whole world rose up against them cruelly on this account. In Germany and other parts of the world where Jews lived, they were massacred and slaughtered by Christians, and many thousands were burned everywhere, indiscriminately. The unshaken if [foolish] constancy of the [Jewish] men and their wives was remarkable. For mothers hurled their children first into the fire that they might not be baptized, and then leapt in after them to burn with their husbands and children. It is said that many bad Christians were burned who in a like manner put poison into wells. But in truth, such poisonings, granted that they actually were perpetrated, could not have caused so great a plague nor infected so many people.[50]

In many areas local authorities protected Jewish communities, but in some places such efforts failed. The town council of Strasbourg tried to protect the local Jewish community, but powerful citizens

A Long, Sad History

The pogroms associated with the Black Death were just one installment in the long history of persecution of Jews in Europe. In A Distant Mirror, *historian Barbara Tuchman discusses persecution of the Jews during the thirteenth century, which set the stage for the fourteenth-century pogroms during the Black Death.*

"Throughout the [thirteenth] century the Church multiplied decrees designed to isolate Jews from Christian society, on the theory that contact with them brought the Christian faith into disrepute. Jews were forbidden to employ Christians as servants, to serve as doctors to Christians, to intermarry, to sell flour, bread, wine, oil, shoes, or any article of clothing to Christians, to deliver or receive goods, to build new synagogues, to hold or claim land for non-payment of mortgage. The occupations from which guild rules barred them included weaving, metal-working, mining, tailoring, shoemaking, goldsmithing, baking, milling, carpentry. To mark their separation, Innocent III in 1215 decreed the wearing of a badge, usually in the form of a wheel or circular patch of yellow felt, said to represent a piece of money. Sometimes green or red-and-white, it was worn by both sexes beginning between the ages of seven and fourteen. . . . A hat with a point rather like a horn, said to represent the Devil, was later added further to distinguish the Jews."

In Basel, the dead are carted off while clergy attend to the dying. The citizens of Basel responded to the plague by persecuting their Jewish population.

in the town replaced the council members, and the townspeople then proceeded to burn all the two thousand Jewish residents.

Pope Clement issued a papal bull (an official document) urging clergy to protect the Jews, commenting that "most of the [flagellants] or their followers, beneath an appearance of piety, set their hands to cruel and impious works, shedding the blood of Jews, whom Christian piety accepts and sustains."[51] In the general hysteria, even the pope's words carried little weight.

Switzerland seemed the most zealous in persecutions. The town of Zurich expelled the entire Jewish community. In Basel, a special building was erected on an island in the Rhine River. The town's Jewish community of about two hundred was locked in the building, which was then burned. The town council then passed a decree banning Jews from settling in Basel for two hundred years.

Through 1348 and 1349, the pogroms continued in Germany, Switzerland, and France, in towns large and small—Brussels, Frankfurt-am-Main, Cologne, Dresden, Stuttgart, Worms, Baden. In Speyer, the bodies of Jewish victims were placed in barrels and floated down the Rhine River. In Mainz, which had a prosperous Jewish community of more than three thousand, the Jews fought back when attacked, killing two hundred Christians. Enraged, the Christian inhabitants of the town gathered reinforcements and completely wiped out the Jews.

As the Black Death moved north and east, violence against Jews went with it. The pogroms ended in the German Rhineland by the close of 1349 and slowly disappeared from the rest of central Europe as the Black Death passed. In eastern Europe, the Black Death was comparatively mild, and there was less violence against the Jews.

Many Jews who survived the pogroms fled to eastern Europe, especially to Poland and Russia. In Poland, King Casimir III welcomed Jewish immigrants and offered them protection. The communities that the Jews established in Poland and Russia during the Black Death flourished for nearly six hundred years until the great Holocaust of the twentieth century.

Chapter

5 The Aftermath of the Black Death

The Black Death ended its terrible journey by late 1351, leaving Europe dramatically depopulated. Although the poor in their crowded quarters were more vulnerable to the plague, the rich and noble died as well. The king of Castile, the queen of Navarre, two successive archbishops of Canterbury, the queen of Burgundy, and the daughter of the king of England all died of plague.

The horrors of the Black Death had a dramatic impact on human behavior and psychology. According to the Italian chronicler Villani, "They forgot the past as though it had never been and gave themselves up to a more disordered and shameful life than they had led before."[52] In England, the numbers of homicides doubled between 1349 and 1369, compared with the number between 1320 and 1340, despite the one-third decrease in population.

Greed and callousness were commonplace as well. Especially scandalous was the defrauding of many orphans of wealthy families. Greedy people married the young survivors who had inherited their families' wealth, or they had themselves appointed the young survivors' guardians and then extorted money from them. In Siena, Italy, officials took steps to stop the practice by forbidding the mar-riage of young females without the consent of relatives.

With so many homes and fields abandoned, peasants took over tools, livestock, and other possessions that had belonged to their fellows or their masters. They moved into abandoned homes, sleeping

As the plague died away, so did people's morals. Even the institution of marriage was affected, as the greedy married those who had inherited fortunes.

on beds perhaps for the first time in their lives. Immediately following the Black Death, there was an abundance of goods and few people left to buy them, and prices fell. Currency was in overabundance, since so many people had died. The result was that survivors went into a frenzy of buying, purchasing luxury goods that they had never before had the opportunity to own.

Changing Values

The Black Death brought a fundamental change in medieval psychology. The sense of cooperation—working together in communities or in guilds for the benefit of all—was replaced by a sense of individualism. People seemed to be left with the feeling that doing their duty and obeying the laws of church and state was no guarantee of security or stability. They believed that human beings were no longer God's favored creatures, and many began to put themselves and their own interests first.

One result of the change was the growth of hedonism—the pursuit of pleasure. If one-third of the world could die in such a short time, who knows what tomorrow might bring? Perhaps the best thing is to live for oneself, to live for the day. In the decade following the Black Death, hedonism reached its peak. In the introduction to *The Decameron*, Giovanni Boccaccio tells of the terrible ravages of the Black Death. Yet the characters of *The Decameron* are ten carefree, well-to-do young men and women of Florence who retire to the country to await the passing of the Black Death. To pass the time, they tell stories.

The values reflected in Boccaccio's stories may have been brewing long before the Black Death, yet the carefree pursuit of pleasure, the cynical attitude toward piety and good works, and the admiration of the clever over the virtuous mark a

Giovanni Boccaccio left a vivid, moving account of the plague's march through Florence. It survives as one of the most well documented primary sources of the Black Death.

change from preplague attitudes. Alongside these attitudes rose attitudes of pessimism and gloom, which would become the dominant theme for over a century. Life was fragile and brief, and in the end all turned to dust. This attitude of pessimism about life and bringing forth new life is exemplified in the work of the French writer Eustace Deschamps:

Happy is he who has no children, for babies mean nothing but crying and stench; they give only trouble and anxiety; they have to be clothed, shod, and fed; they are always in danger of falling and hurting themselves; they contract some illness and die. When they grow up, they may go bad and be put in prison. Nothing but cares and sorrows; no happiness compensates us for our anxiety, for the trouble and expense of their education. The poet has no word.[53]

Changing Images in Art

Before the Black Death, art reflected the virtues of Christianity—love, kindness, forgiveness. The Virgin Mary and child Jesus are portrayed often, bathed in heavenly light, surrounded by angels. Although people accepted death as inevitable, it was not a preoccupation.

Following the Black Death, images in art changed dramatically. Macabre images of death and judgment often depicted devils torturing souls in hell. Death was often personified as a grisly skeleton, sometimes holding a scythe (a sharp tool used to cut wheat) and an hourglass. In a well-known fresco (a painting on plaster, often on the walls of a church) painted by Italian artist Triani about 1350, a group of beautiful and noble young men and ladies amuse themselves in an orange grove, unaware that overhead Death is swooping toward them. Nearby lies a pile of corpses; bodies of the poor are stacked in a heap with bodies of knights, a pope, and royalty. A scroll below the painting warns observers that neither riches nor nobility nor wisdom can protect them from death.

The World Has Not Changed for the Better

According to the French friar Jean de Venette, following the Black Death many women gave birth to twins and even triplets. However, in his Chronicle *Friar Jean concludes that the birth of a new generation did not rid the world of sin.*

"But woe is me! the world has not changed for the better but for the worse by this renewal of population. For men were more [greedy] and grasping than before, even though they had far greater possessions. They were more covetous and disturbed each other more frequently with [law]suits, brawls, disputes, and pleas. Nor by the mortality resulting from this terrible plague inflicted by God was peace between kings and lords established. On the contrary, the enemies of the king of France and of the Church were stronger and wickeder than before and stirred up wars on sea and on land. Greater evils than before [sprouted] everywhere in the world."

The Black Death led to more gruesome and bleak depictions of life. Here death hacks away at the tree of life.

Social Change

The Black Death brought changes not only to the psychology and behavior of medieval people but also to the trifunctional social order. The manorial system, which was already crumbling before the Black Death, rapidly disintegrated. The growing strength of the middle class, associated with increased trade and expanding prosperity, and the decline in the need of a permanent warrior class due to an era of peace in Europe had posed problems for the nobles long before the Black Death. Wealthy merchants, envious of the status of nobility, often used their wealth as a leverage to marry into titled families. Consequently, to maintain their family lines, the aristocracy needed to produce male heirs to their lands and titles. Producing offspring that survived to adulthood was

Failure of the Church

Chroniclers throughout Europe agreed upon one thing—the clergy failed in their sacred duty to their flocks. The church's failure in the crisis of the Black Death was a factor in hastening the Reformation, which began in earnest a century and a half later. In his book Medieval Panorama, *historian G. G. Coulton sums up the evidence against the clergy.*

"We have the judgment of 22 chroniclers . . . upon the behaviour of the clergy during the pestilence. Of the eight least unfavourable, one only is entirely favourable; but he speaks only for his own neighbourhood (Catania). The two next best, while praising the friars or the nurses, contrast these with the negligent behaviour of parish priests. The remainder are frankly, and sometimes violently, unfavourable. It would be difficult to find any historical question, involving so directly and so deeply the reputation of [such a large] and influential body [as the church], with exceptional [resources] for self-defence and self-advertisement, in which the evidence is so overwhelming against them. Even [if] all these chroniclers had been mistaken as to the facts . . . there would still remain the plain consideration that, whatever the priests had actually done, public opinion did judge them to have fallen, as a body, far below the height of their sacred office. That belief, in itself, would go far to explain . . . the Reformation."

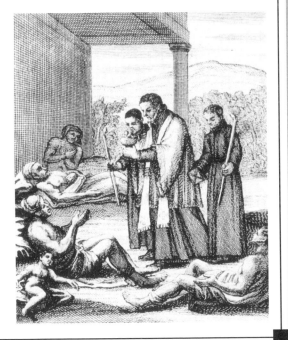

While these priests do their duty, administering communion to dying plague victims, many fell short, often abandoning their flock in order to save themselves.

difficult enough during the Middle Ages, given all the mishaps of accident and disease that could befall a child, and the Black Death was a death knell for many family lines.

Along with the aristocracy two other solid institutions, the church and the lord's manor, were shaken to the roots by the effects of the Black Death.

The Church Loses Prestige

Survivors of the Black Death were disappointed that the clergy as a whole had failed to intercede with God to stop the plague and that individual members had failed in their obligations to their flocks. Traditionally the clergy were believed to have special powers as intermediaries between God and human beings, but following the Black Death people began to seek salvation through other means. Christianity remained a dominant force in their lives, but many people began to believe they did not need clergy to lead them to salvation. They began to think of themselves as having an individual relationship with God, without the need for a priest intermediary.

The Black Death made people even more aware of the need for salvation. People began to undertake a variety of good works that required no involvement of priests, such as giving money to hospitals or poor monasteries. Going on pilgrimages was considered one of the most important good works for the salvation of the soul. The poor and the well-off alike undertook difficult and often dangerous journeys to faraway places such as Rome or Jerusalem or to local shrines that con-

The plague led to widespread dissatisfaction with the church. If the church had the ear of God, why could it not stop the plague, many wondered.

tained relics of saints. Pilgrimages became so popular that travel guidebooks describing the journey and highlights along the way were in high demand. Another avenue to salvation was mysticism, in which pious laypeople practiced prayer and self-denial. The mystics believed that God was present in the soul of everyone and that by quieting the sensual appetites, one could communicate with God directly, without the services of a priest.

Although the church suffered an enormous loss of prestige during the Black Death, the people remained deeply tied to Christianity and were more thirsty than ever for spiritual values in an uncertain and frightening world.

A local church displays its collection of relics in a procession. Many pilgrims traveled great distances to visit shrines that contained such relics as a piece of the cross upon which Jesus was crucified.

One cannot claim that these trends toward reliance on individual conscience, which had emerged before the Black Death, led directly to the Reformation, which erupted a little more than a century and a half later. Even without the Black Death, the church most likely would have been forced into some reform. Nevertheless, the spiritual upheavals caused by the Black Death almost certainly hastened the coming of the Reformation.

The Lord's Manor and Labor Shortages

The loss of overwhelming numbers of people naturally led to immediate and dramatic labor shortages, and this economic situation provided a direct benefit to the peasants. Agricultural products were abundant, eliminating the food shortages of the early part of the century and depressing the prices for agricultural goods. The English chronicler Henry Knighton describes the situation:

> There were small prices for virtually everything. A man could have a horse, which was worth 40 shillings, for 6 shillings, 8 pence, a cow for 12 pence. . . . Sheep and cattle went wandering over fields and through crops, and there was no one to drive or gather them together.[54]

With a greatly diminished labor force, the cost of labor rose. The trend toward freeing peasants from their bondage to the land had begun long before the Black Death struck. Now peasants who were freemen working for wages demanded higher wages; peasants who had not yet freed themselves from the labor required by the lord insisted that the landlord give them freedom and pay them wages. Landlords who refused found themselves without laborers—peasants slipped away to a city or found another manor lord who would pay higher wages.

The standard of living for the average peasant was rising at a remarkable rate. As agricultural prices fell, wages continued to rise. Meanwhile, the landed classes—the nobility and clergy—were having more and more difficulty keeping workers. As prices fell, the value of land itself declined. The landlords made an effort to contain the situation and maintain the old order of society by passing laws to keep wages low and workers tied to the land. In 1349 France passed a Statute of Labor capping wages at pre-1348 rates. England passed a Statute of Labourers in 1351 with the same goal. Workers who refused to work or who left an employer to seek higher wages were subject to fines. By 1360 imprisonment was added to the penalties. In England fugitive laborers could be branded with an *F* on their forehead, for "fugitive."

The laws could not be enforced, however, and landowners soon found that the only way to keep laborers was to pay the wages they demanded, in some cases two or three times the preplague rates. Marginal lands were allowed to return to their natural state or turned to pasture, since the cost of labor for cultivation was so high. Consequently, the nobility faced a major reduction in income. In England, incomes of aristocratic landholders fell more than 20 percent between 1347 and 1353.

Depopulation caused by the plague was the death blow to the manorial system. The lord still held the land, but the peasants were no longer serfs tied to it; they were renters. By 1500, most peasants in western Europe held long-term leases on as much land as they could farm. For the landlords, depopulation spelled economic crisis. As demand for agricultural products dropped, many landlords ceased trying to cultivate their land and simply leased it out. Others turned to animal husbandry—raising sheep and cattle. Lords with large landholdings especially favored sheep because of the high demand for mutton and wool for the textile mills. Smaller landholders resorted to dairy farming. In some parts of Europe, especially France, Italy, and Spain, viticulture—the cultivation of grapes for wine—was introduced or expanded.

A lord hands out assignments to serfs. The Black Death helped end the system of feudalism because few people were left to labor in the fields.

In an effort to keep workers and merchants in their place, special laws, called sumptuary laws, were passed to govern how people dressed. Medieval people believed that clothing and adornment should reflect the class status of the individual. For example, before the Black Death, English law forbade the wearing of fur except by aristocrats and clergy with a certain income. But with the rise in incomes, more people could afford luxurious clothing. The English, attempting to keep some control of the display of wealth by those of lower social standing, passed revised sumptuary laws: Everyone except the poorest workmen could wear fur, but only certain kinds—according to their rank. Wealthy aristocrats could wear the finest quality full-length furs; merchants of high income could wear fine furs, but only on their hoods; less prosperous merchants and craftsmen could wear lambskin; and the poorer could wear rabbit, fox, or cat. The poorest workmen were forbidden to wear any fur. Again, these laws failed to do anything but incite resentment and encourage social climbers to buy the most expensive furs they could possibly afford, regardless of their income and the laws.

All these measures failed to prop up the tottering trifunctional system. Too many changes had taken place. The workers resented the efforts of the nobility and clergy to maintain the status quo, which ultimately led to violent uprisings.

The Revolts of the Rural Peasants

The rising level of wages and the attempt by the landed classes to maintain the old system through legislation resulted in worker uprisings—peasant uprisings in England and France and an urban workers' uprising in Italy. Tensions had been growing before the Black Death, but the plague and events that followed contributed to the bloody confrontations.

The Hundred Years' War between France and England raged on with barely a pause for the Black Death; French peasants were the targets of knights-turned-brigands, called freebooters, who roamed the countryside, pillaging the peasants' belongings and sometimes taking their lives. French nobles did little or nothing to protect the peasants from attack, but the nobles continued to demand extra taxes to ransom captive nobles from the English. In 1356 the English captured the king of France at the battle of Poitiers. Angry peasants, loyal to the king and despising the nobles, were convinced that the nobles had allowed the king to be captured.

In May 1358, angry peasants met in a village near Senlis. Declaring that the knights were good for nothing but oppressing the peasants, they took up arms to destroy the aristocrats. The uprising became known as the Jacquerie, an insulting term taken from the word *jacques*, which referred to the leather vest peasants wore in battle. Armed only with staves and knives, a group attacked the nearest manor and killed the knight and his family. Following that, according to the chronicler Jean Froissart:

They went to a strong castle, tied the knight to a stake while his wife and daughter were raped by many, one after another before his eyes; then they killed the wife who was pregnant and afterward the daughter and all the children and lastly the knight and burned and destroyed the castle.[55]

Froissart received his information from nobles and clergy who may well have exaggerated the stories; nevertheless, the Jacquerie was a bloody uprising inspired by hatred. The uprising gathered strength and numbers; its center was at the heart of France in the valleys of the Seine and Loire Rivers. Despite the horror stories, the peasants engaged mainly in looting and destruction of property. Charles of Navarre, a noble who had designs on the French throne, raised troops to put down the uprising. Chroniclers claim thousands of peasant fighters were killed in battle and thousands more were hunted down and savagely murdered, although these numbers are doubtlessly exaggerated. Nevertheless, the revolt ended with much bloodshed after less than a month, leaving little changed.

The Hundred Years' War continued throughout the plague years.

After the Jacqueries are defeated, the dead and dying are thrown into the river.

Revolt of the Urban Workers

In Italy, the same social tensions existed between worker and employer, but in an urban setting. In Florence, the textile workers, who were known as *ciompi*, were held in contempt by the ruling elite of bankers and traders, and the workers had little say in their own affairs. During the 1370s, the textile market suffered a brief setback, and the currency in which the workers were paid, the penny, was devalued. The ruling elite kept their money in florins, a more stable currency. By 1378, the penny had dropped to about one-fourth its value in 1349, and the workers' standard of living dropped dramatically. The florin, however, maintained its value; consequently, the wealthy rulers did not suffer an economic reversal.

Violence broke out in the summer of 1378. Rioting workers broke into houses and palaces of the rich, looting and destroying. This uprising of *ciompi* resulted in some gains; the workers were allowed guilds of their own, tax reform, and a voice in government. However, the textile crisis ran its course by 1383, and the workers lost much of their gains. Nevertheless, they were able to maintain a stable wage thereafter.

The Peasants' Revolt in England

The best known of the rebellions following the Black Death is the 1381 Peasants' Revolt in England. As was the case elsewhere in Europe, resentments against landlords had long been smoldering. In the decades that followed the Black Death, the surviving workers began to get a new sense of their own worth and friction grew between landlords and peasants. The peasants demanded higher wages and more freedom of movement. The landed classes resisted the change and continued to attempt to cap worker wages and to deny the peasants freedom to move to other manors. The final straw was an unfair poll tax imposed on peasants. A poll tax, sometimes called a head tax, is a set amount of tax levied on each citizen, no matter how poor. Thus every individual peasant was required to pay the same amount as the wealthy landlords paid. In Essex in eastern England, peasants refused to pay the tax and drove tax collectors out of their town. A spontaneous revolt erupted, and riots broke out across England in which property was destroyed and landowners killed.

In June, a blacksmith named Wat Tyler led a peasant army on a march to London. By the time the angry army reached the city, nearly 100,000 peasants had joined Tyler's band. The peasants demanded to see the king. When King Richard II, who was only fourteen years old at the time, refused to meet with them, the peasants rioted in the city of London, looting, killing, and destroying and burning property. A group led by Tyler captured the Tower of London and killed the archbishop of Canterbury. Finally, Richard agreed to meet

Complaint of the Laborers

The Black Death caused an enormous labor shortage. Remaining laborers demanded and received higher wages, despite laws that were passed to freeze wages. This dramatic rise in the standard of living led even beggars to be choosers. In Piers the Ploughman, *written not long after the Black Death, the English poet William Langland describes the situation.*

"And then Waster would not work any more, but set out as a tramp. And the beggars refused the bread that had beans in it, demanding milk loaves and fine white wheaten bread. And they would not drink cheap beer at any price, but only the best brown ale that is sold in the towns.

And the day-labourers, who have no land to live on but their shovels, would not deign to eat yesterday's vegetables. And draught-ale was not good enough for them, nor a hunk of bacon, but they must have fresh meat or fish, fried or baked. . . .

And so it is nowadays—the labourer is angry unless he gets high wages, and he curses the day that he was ever born a workman. . . . He blames God, and murmurs against Reason, and curses the king and his Council for making Statutes [laws] on purpose to plague the workmen!"

Peasant leader Wat Tyler is killed in a scuffle while he talks with King Richard II. Without Tyler's leadership, the Peasants' Revolt ended.

with the leaders of the mob. The chronicler Froissart reports the meeting:

> The King . . . showed great courage, and on his arrival at the appointed spot instantly advanced into the midst of the assembled multitude, saying in a most pleasing manner, "My good people, I am your king and your lord, what is it you want? What do you wish to say to me?" Those who heard him made answer, "We wish you to make us free for ever. We wish to be no longer called slaves, nor held in bondage." The King replied, "I grant your wish; now therefore return to your homes . . . I will order letters to be given with my seal, fully granting every demand you have made."[56]

With that, most of the mob disbanded, but Tyler and some thirty thousand peasants remained near London, trying to gain more concessions. The next day Tyler met with the king and the mayor of London, and Tyler was killed in a scuffle. Upon arrival of the king's troops, the remaining mob scattered to return home. The Peasants' Revolt was over. However, the rebels had made some permanent gains: The poll tax was eliminated, and no more laws were passed to cap wages or limit the peasants' movements. By 1400, the old manorial system had almost entirely disappeared.

Chapter

6 Europe Transformed

In the decade following the Black Death, people began to forget the horror of the plague, daily life began to return to normal, and the population began to recover. As chronicler Jean de Venette remarks:

> After the cessation of the epidemic, pestilence, or plague, the men and women who survived married each other. There was no sterility among the women, but on the contrary fertility beyond the ordinary. Pregnant women were seen on every side. Many twins were born and even three children at once.[57]

Had these high marriage and birth rates of the 1350s continued, along with low death rates, the population would have been near preplague levels by 1380. But the Black Death was just the beginning of a centuries-long plague pandemic.

Pestis Secunda: A Continuing Nightmare

In 1361 the second plague visitation appeared, sometimes called the *pestis secunda*. As is the nature of the plague, once established in an area, it will continue to recur. The second epidemic was primarily bubonic and not as severe as the Black Death; still, it was one of the deadliest epidemics in history. A third epidemic struck in 1369, only slightly less severe. With a few exceptions, later epidemics were less severe, but they

Even though people did not die in the vast numbers that they had during the first visitation of the plague, many died in the epidemics that reappeared periodically over the following centuries.

The Great Plague of London

One of the last great outbreaks of plague struck London in 1665. Daniel Defoe (famous for his novel Robinson Crusoe) *wrote an account of that plague entitled* A Journal of the Plague Year. *Although the account is fictionalized, Defoe was a child during the epidemic and recalled many details of the plague. According to his account, medical science was still trying the same cures that were used during the Black Death, but apparently doctors were performing autopsies.*

"The pain of the swelling was in particular very violent and to some intolerable; the physicians and surgeons may be said to have tortured many poor creatures even to death. The swellings in some grew hard, and they applied violent drawing-plaisters or poultices to break them, and if these did not do they cut and scarified them in a terrible manner. In some those swellings . . . were so hard that no instrument could cut them, and then they burnt them with causticks, so that many people died raving mad with the torment, and some in the very operation. In these distresses, some, for want of help to hold them down in their beds, or to look to them, laid hands upon themselves [killed themselves]. . . . [Others] would be taken suddenly very sick and would run to a bench . . . or to their own houses if possible . . . and there sit down, grow faint, and die. . . . Such as died thus had very little notice of their being infected at all till the gangreen was spread through their whole body; nor could physicians themselves know certainly how it was with them, till they opened their breasts or other parts of their body and saw the [signs of the plague]."

Corpses are piled into carts during the London plague of 1665.

Reapers harvest wheat. To keep peasants on the land, eastern Europe introduced serfdom only after the Black Death.

continued to recur every few years, through the fifteenth century, killing many of those born between epidemics before they reached reproductive age. The succeeding epidemics were usually not as widespread as the Black Death. Nevertheless, the overall effect was not only to deplete the population further but also to prevent population recovery. Historians estimate that between 1349 and 1450, the total population of Europe declined an astonishing 60 to 75 percent. After about 1500, intervals between epidemics increased, allowing the population to begin to increase. However, the depopulation begun during the Black Death and continued in succeeding plague epidemics led to major transformations in Europe.

A Changing Land

The most visible change brought by massive depopulation was the way in which land was used, and ultimately, the end of the manorial system. Much of the marginal land was abandoned or turned to pasture lands, as manor lords concentrated on cultivating the most fertile lands. A dramatic effect of this abandonment was the regrowth of old grasslands and ancient forests that had been cleared in the twelfth and thirteenth centuries. With the forests came the wildlife that had once been pushed back to the outer limits of European civilization. In the 1420s, wolves were seen roaming the outskirts of Paris, an event that chroniclers of the time felt was unusual enough to record. In the 1470s, an English historian, John Rous, traveled through western England and commented on the fifty-eight lost villages that he had observed: "If such destruction as that in Warwickshire took place in other parts of the country, it would be a national danger."[58]

The depopulation caused by the plague pandemic that began with the Black Death may have been a disaster for human society, but it was a positive event for the environment of much of Europe. Today, most of the forests that cover Europe originated in the period following the Black Death.

Unfortunately for the peasants of eastern Europe, their land was especially fertile and suitable for growing wheat. As western European landholders began to diversify in their use of land, eastern Europe became the breadbasket for the continent. Wheat farming was labor intensive, however, and required large numbers of laborers whose wages could be kept low and who could be kept tied to the land. In some areas of eastern Europe, serfdom was actually introduced for the first time following the Black Death. Landlords used force to keep peasants in their place, and serfdom continued in some regions of eastern Europe for more than four hundred years.

A traveler through Britain and Europe in 1500 would find a far different land than was found in the early 1300s, when villages were scattered over the landscape and every scrap of land was under cultivation. By 1500 great forests grew where villages once stood; large herds of sheep or cattle roamed over land once planted in wheat. While the cities flourished, in the countryside there were far fewer people,

and in western Europe, those people were free, no longer the serfs of some great landlord. Industrious descendants of one-time serfs were prosperous, even rich. In contrast, in eastern Europe, descendants of free people who had once migrated east in search of more land were now serfs, tied to the land and to the misery of serfdom for several centuries to come.

Industry and Economy

Depopulation had a lasting effect on the commercial lives of Europeans. Because the market for many staple goods diminished greatly, specialized products were developed. People who had more money were interested in living more luxuriously

From Villein to Landlord

As the manorial system broke down, peasants willing to work hard could dramatically change their circumstances. In Europe in Transition, *Wallace K. Ferguson quotes a medieval account of an English peasant, Clement Paston, whose descendants became wealthy landowners.*

"He was a good plain [man], and lived upon his land that he had in Paston, and kept thereon a plough all times in the year, and sometimes in barleysell two ploughs. The said Clement [went] at one plough both winter and summer, and he rode to mill on the bare horseback with his corn under him, and brought home meal again under him; and also drove his cart with [various grains] to Wynterton to sell, as a good [man] ought to do. Also he had in Paston a five score or a six score acres of land at the most [about four times a normal villein holding], and much thereof bondland to Gemyngham Hall, with a little poor water-mill running by the river there."

Once the Black Death had subsided, the wealthy wanted to live more luxuriously. Here, servants attend to a lady while she lies in her bedroom. Her child, left, is attended by a nursemaid.

than they had before the plague. Prior to the Black Death, Flemish textile producers had turned out inexpensive, plain woolen cloth for the mass market. After the Black Death, although there were fewer people to buy cloth, many of the survivors wanted something better—rich brocades, silk, and fine linen. The latter was required for the newest fashion innovation—underwear. Consequently, Flemish textile producers suffered, but those who could make the change to producing or importing luxury items prospered.

European entrepreneurs were quick to take advantage of people's thirst for luxury items. English merchants shipped cloth and other goods across the European continent. From the 1400s to the 1600s, Dutch, English, and Iberian merchants established all-water routes to markets once laboriously traveled over-land and opened trade routes to lands unheard-of before the Black Death.

Education and the Mother Tongue

The Black Death also had a dramatic effect on higher education. Many of Europe's most important scholars and thinkers, as well as many faculty of the universities, died during the plague. Students at the university in Avignon in France complained to the pope:

> The university body of your studium at Avignon is deprived of all lectures, since the whole number has been left desolate by the death of pestilence of doctors, licentiates [teachers], bachelors, and students.[59]

A teacher leads pupils in a daily lesson. Clerical schools declined after the Black Death had devastated the population, and secular schools were founded.

A primary mission of the universities had been to provide training for the clergy. So many clergy had been lost in the Black Death that training new clergy was imperative. At Cambridge, in England, the colleges of Trinity Hall, Gonville Hill, and Corpus Christi were founded to help train priests; likewise at Oxford, the college that is still called New College was founded in 1379.

The problem of training new clergy was not so easily solved, however; the secondary or grammar schools, which prepared students for the university, had suffered from the general depopulation as well. The grammar of grammar schools was Latin, the language of the church. Many of the priests who had taught in grammar school were transferred to universities to train young men for the priesthood. People who replaced the transferred instructors in the grammar schools were often ill equipped to teach Latin, and sometimes completely incompetent. In France, the chronicler Jean de Venette complained that "few were found in houses, villas and castles who were able and willing to instruct boys in grammar."[60] Thus, many young men came to the university ill prepared. Ultimately, this spelled the decline of scholasticism, the philosophical and theological traditions based on the early Latin church fathers and on the ideas of Aristotle.

A dramatic and long-lasting change in language occurred in England, where Latin and French had been the official languages of government since the Norman Conquest of the eleventh century. As a result of the death of large numbers of officials who were fluent in those languages, English was proclaimed the official language of the government. As a result, the use of French quickly died out, and by 1385 an English schoolmaster commented that "nowadays boys know no more French than their left heel."[61]

Education suffered setbacks from the Black Death and the following depopulation, yet many historians believe this was not all bad. Ultimately, the loss of many of the clerical scholastics with their sometimes rigid and dogmatic approach to learning opened the way for a new wave of thought. Humanism, which was the intellectual and cultural movement that concerned itself with human beings and emphasized the secular over the spiritual, was the foundation of thought for the coming age of the Renaissance.

Making Medicine a Science

Medieval medicine failed miserably in the face of the Black Death. Guy de Chauliac, the personal physician to Pope Clement and one of the most successful and prestigious physicians of the time, writes:

> The plague [was] shameful for physicians, who could give no help at all, es-

pecially as, out of fear of infection, they hesitated to visit the sick. Even if they did they achieved nothing, and earned no fees, for all those who caught the plague died, except for a few towards the end of the epidemic who escaped after the buboes had ripened.[62]

This massive failure marked the beginning of the professionalization of medicine, one of the most far-reaching consequences of the Black Death. To be sure, modern medicine was centuries away, but the abysmal failure of medieval medicine to understand and control the plague, and to treat plague victims, led to profound changes in medical study and medical practice. Medical study of the time was based on logical analysis of the classical ancient medical texts of the Greek physicians Hippocrates and Galen, and on the Arab

A physician tends to a plague victim. Medieval medicine failed to curb the spread of the Black Death; ironically, this failure brought about drastic changes in the study of medicine and medical practice.

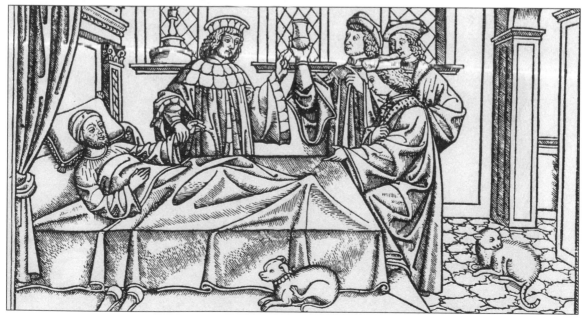

Chivalry and the Aristocrat

As old aristocratic families died out and the wealthy merchants bought their way into aristocratic titles, the aristocracy tried to maintain their identity as a class by renewing their interest in chivalry. In his book The Civilization of the Middle Ages, *Norman Cantor explains the role chivalry played for the aristocracy.*

"Aristocratic court life in the fifteenth century became extremely stylized and immensely more expensive with [great numbers] of rituals, games, pageants, and feasts. On the imagined model of King Arthur's Knights of the Round Table, kings and dukes established tightly selected orders of chivalry carrying titles like Order of the Garter and Knights of the Golden Fleece. A great deal of time [and] money, and artistic, costuming, and cuisinary ingenuity was devoted to the ceremonial activities of these privileged orders. Tournaments were no longer loosely organized war games. They were now minutely choreographed exhibitions of individual prowess. . . .

The aristocratic chivalric displays of the latter Middle Ages were intended to give to the life-style of the higher nobility an intrinsic social value so that the vast expense, thought, and imagination and the best artistic skills lavished on their life-style were justifiably expended. This was the way the nobility blocked [their decline in status] in the face of the [enormous wealth] and leisure time of the great merchants and some governmental officials of [common] lineage."

Although the system of feudalism declined after the Black Death, tournaments of skill, such as this one, became more stylized and elaborate.

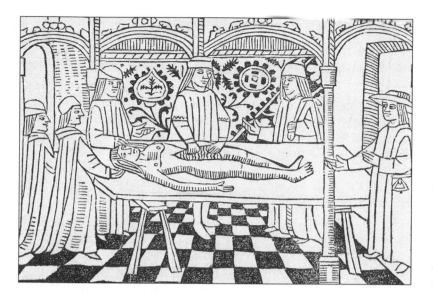

A professor of medicine lectures to his students during an autopsy on a cadaver. Once cadavers were allowed to be dissected, physicians' knowledge of anatomy greatly improved.

commentators on these texts. Clinical research and observation, actual hands-on study of patients, was not practiced.

The church maintained control of most education, including medical training, and imposed its theological standards on the practice of medicine. One particular act that curtailed medical investigation was a papal bull issued in 1300 by Pope Boniface VIII forbidding mutilation of dead bodies. The pope wanted to stop grave robbers searching for valuables, but the effect was to halt dissection and the subsequent learning about anatomy and disease.

Many of the prominent physicians teaching at the universities died during the plague, leaving the field open to new ideas. At the University of Paris, the medical faculty shrank from forty-six in 1348 to twenty in 1387. Throughout Europe, prominent physicians and medical writers perished. The generation who took their places were all too aware of the failure of traditional medicine and in many cases were eager to make changes.

One of the most important changes was that the dissection of cadavers, which had formerly been banned, began to be practiced regularly. By the 1380s knowledge of anatomy was fairly accurate, and the emphasis began to shift from theoretical to practical knowledge. As a result, the scientific method of postulating a theory and then testing it through observation was developed, which opened the way for a professional approach to medicine and to scientific investigation in later centuries.

Following the Black Death, surgery became an important part of the medical curriculum at the universities in northern Europe, which had previously excluded surgeons. Prior to the Black Death, surgeons were considered craftsmen who set broken bones, closed wounds, and practiced bleeding patients. By 1400 surgeons had become a part of the medical elite, enjoying a status nearly equal with that of physicians.

Hospitals took on a new role following the Black Death. They began to form associations with doctors and universities and became places of healing rather than

Medieval How-To Medicine

Disillusioned by the failure of established medicine, people turned to popular how-to medical books, from which the following recipe for delivering a stillborn child is taken. The quote is excerpted from The Black Death *by Robert Gottfried.*

"Take leek blades and scale them and bind them to the womb about the navel; and it shall cast out the dead child; and when she [the mother] is delivered, take away the blades or she shall cast out all that is in her."

A medieval apothecary offers medicine to a client. Such medicines rarely worked.

places where the sick could be confined until they died.

Another important change was the development of a code of ethics for doctors. Guy de Chauliac describes how a professional physician should behave.

> The doctor should be well mannered, bold in many ways, fearful of dangers, that he should abhore the false cures or practices. He should be affable to the sick, kindhearted to his colleagues, wise in his prognostications. He should be chaste, sober, compassionate, and merciful; he should not be covetous, grasping in money matters,

and then he will receive a salary commensurate with his labors, the financial ability of his patients, the success of the treatment, and his own dignity.[63]

Prior to the Black Death, medieval medicine was an antiquated system that had little to say about infectious diseases and could offer little practical help in easing the suffering of plague victims. The Black Death forced the medical establishment to take a practical hands-on approach to medicine, exemplified in the new status of surgeons, and to develop the scientific method in approaching illness, rather than relying upon ancient medical texts.

Epilogue

The Legacy of the Black Death

The immediate impact of the Black Death was the loss of one-third to one-half the population of Europe in about four years. Some areas may have experienced much higher death tolls. In most areas, the great dying took place in the space of a few months, as the plague moved across the face of the continent. As shocking as this was to the people, the impact was dramatically compounded by the continuing outbreaks of the plague. In the face of this terrible and mysterious onslaught, helpless people began to question their most deeply held beliefs.

Our modern world is in part a product of the issues raised by the Black Death. First, our sense of individualism, which is the primary mark of human beings in the modern world, began to take shape in response to the Black Death. Prior to the plague, medieval society was based, ideally at least, on a hierarchical social and economic order in which everyone participated according to their assigned place in society, which was fixed at birth. People shared a sense of material and spiritual community and a sense of certainty about the here and the hereafter. Eternal life was the most important consideration. If some individuals enjoyed many material benefits in this world, those who suffered at the bottom of the hierarchy would re-

ceive their reward in heaven. God was just. In any case, people did not seriously question the world order, since it was ordained and directed by God.

The Black Death led to a moral crisis. What had the human race done that God would punish people so fiercely? Had humanity lost its place as the jewel of God's

A priest performs last rites on a plague victim while corpses, including those of other priests, litter the ground. The Black Death resulted in the loss of one-third of the population of Europe.

A medieval marketplace teems with activity. The Black Death hastened the decline in the hierarchy of royalty and peasants. It was replaced with a sense of individualism which continues to drive society today.

creation? Why could neither physician nor priest appease the wrath of God? If God Himself would act in such an arbitrary manner, destroying millions in such a horrible way, what in the world or in eternity could be counted upon?

As the plague continued its apparent random appearances medieval certainties began to unravel; questions were raised and left unanswered. Human beings were set adrift. They no longer felt part of a society whose order was fixed and constant and ordained by God. They began to think as individuals. Serfs no longer felt tied to the hierarchical community that was the manor. Peasants and merchants alike began to be concerned with providing for themselves in this world, no longer entirely certain about what awaited them in the next. Penance and a last con-

fession no longer guaranteed a place in heaven. Hell began to loom large in people's imaginations. More important, individuals no longer trusted the priests to intercede on their behalf; people began to take charge of their own spiritual lives, seeking God in their own ways. The new attitude of individualism developed gradually. Medieval society did not become modern society overnight, but the Black Death hastened the emergence of individualism that gradually transformed medieval society.

Second, the attitude toward nature and toward medicine that is a mark of our modern world took shape in the age following the Black Death. Out of death rose a new interest in life and how life worked. Old authorities and old tools were abandoned in favor of new approaches to understanding nature and the human body and its ailments. New tools and techniques were tried, and from these early efforts the first glimmerings of modern science arose. The new learning emphasized empirical observation and the experimental, hands-on approach to understanding nature.

These new attitudes toward the individual and toward nature are just two of the many changes brought on by or has-tened by the terrible period of horror and uncertainty that was the Black Death. People began to question and to transform their beliefs and values, their way of life, their reason for being, and their institutions. The thirteenth and fourteenth centuries were, as historian Norman Cantor explains, "an age of transition in which an old world was dying and a new world was struggling to be born."[64] The Black Death was a major turning point in this struggle.

Notes

Introduction: The Great Catastrophe

1. Quoted in Robert Gottfried, *The Black Death*. New York: The Free Press, 1983.

Chapter 1: Europe Before the Black Death

2. Quoted in Georges Duby, *The Three Orders: Feudal Society Imagined*, trans. Arthur Goldhammer. Chicago: University of Chicago Press, 1980.

3. Quoted in Duby, *The Three Orders: Feudal Society Imagined*.

4. Quoted in Norman F. Cantor, *The Civilization of the Middle Ages*. New York: HarperCollins, 1993.

5. Cantor, *The Civilization of the Middle Ages*.

6. Denys Hay, *Europe in the Fourteenth and Fifteenth Centuries*. London: Longman, 1966.

7. Gottfried, *The Black Death*.

Chapter 2: The Black Death Begins

8. Quoted in Gottfried, *The Black Death*.

9. Quoted in Philip Ziegler, *The Black Death*. New York: John Day Company, 1969.

10. Quoted in Ziegler, *The Black Death*.

11. Giovanni Boccaccio, *The Decameron*, trans. G. H. McWilliam. New York: Penguin Books, 1983.

12. Boccaccio, *The Decameron*.

13. Boccaccio, *The Decameron*.

14. Boccaccio, *The Decameron*.

15. Boccaccio, *The Decameron*.

16. Quoted in Derek Turner, *The Black Death*. Essex, UK: Longman, 1978.

17. Quoted in Ziegler, *The Black Death*.

18. Quoted in Ziegler, *The Black Death*.

Chapter 3: The Black Death Sweeps Europe

19. Jean de Venette, *The Chronicle of Jean de Venette*, trans. Jean Birdsall. New York: Columbia University Press, 1953.

20. Quoted in Gottfried, *The Black Death*.

21. Quoted in Ziegler, *The Black Death*.

22. Quoted in Gottfried, *The Black Death*.

23. Quoted in Gottfried, *The Black Death*.

24. Quoted in Ziegler, *The Black Death*.

25. Quoted in Barbara Tuchman, *A Distant Mirror: The Calamitous 14th Century*. New York: Alfred A. Knopf, 1978.

26. Quoted in Tuchman, *A Distant Mirror: The Calamitous 14th Century*.

27. Quoted in Timothy Biel, *The Black Death*. San Diego: Lucent Books, 1989.

28. Quoted in Gottfried, *The Black Death*.

29. de Venette, *The Chronicle of Jean de Venette*.

30. Quoted in Ziegler, *The Black Death*.

31. Quoted in Tuchman, *A Distant Mirror: The Calamitous 14th Century*.

32. Tuchman, *A Distant Mirror: The Calamitous 14th Century*.

33. Quoted in Tuchman, *A Distant Mirror: The Calamitous 14th Century*.

34. Boccaccio, *The Decameron*.

35. Quoted in Ziegler, *The Black Death*.

36. Quoted in Ziegler, *The Black Death*.

37. Quoted in Tuchman, *A Distant Mirror: The Calamitous 14th Century*.

38. Quoted in Henry Sigerist, *Civilization and Disease*. Ithaca, NY: Cornell University Press, 1943.

Chapter 4: Potions, Penance, and Pogroms: The Search for Answers

39. Boccaccio, *The Decameron.*

40. Quoted in Ziegler, *The Black Death.*

41. Quoted in Gottfried, *The Black Death.*

42. Quoted in Daniel Cohen, *The Black Death.* New York: Franklin Watts, 1974.

43. Quoted in Ziegler, *The Black Death.*

44. Quoted in Cohen, *The Black Death.*

45. Quoted in Tuchman, *A Distant Mirror: The Calamitous 14th Century.*

46. Quoted in Norman Cohn, *The Pursuit of the Millennium.* New York: Oxford University Press, 1970.

47. Quoted in Cohn, *The Pursuit of the Millennium.*

48. Cohn, *The Pursuit of the Millennium.*

49. Quoted in Cohn, *The Pursuit of the Millennium.*

50. de Venette, *The Chronicle of Jean de Venette.*

51. Quoted in Gottfried, *The Black Death.*

Chapter 5: The Aftermath of the Black Death

52. Quoted in Tuchman, *A Distant Mirror: The Calamitous 14th Century.*

53. Quoted in Gottfried, *The Black Death.*

54. Quoted in Gottfried, *The Black Death.*

55. Quoted in Tuchman, *A Distant Mirror: The Calamitous 14th Century.*

56. Jean Froissart, *Chronicles of England, France, and Spain,* trans. Thomas Johnes. New York: E. P. Dutton, 1911.

Chapter 6: Europe Transformed

57. de Venette, *The Chronicle of Jean de Venette.*

58. Quoted in Gottfried, *The Black Death.*

59. Quoted in Gottfried, *The Black Death.*

60. Quoted in Tuchman, *A Distant Mirror: The Calamitous 14th Century.*

61. Quoted in Gottfried, *The Black Death.*

62. Quoted in Ziegler, *The Black Death.*

63. Quoted in Gottfried, *The Black Death.*

64. Cantor, *The Civilization of the Middle Ages.*

For Further Reading

Timothy Biel, *The Black Death*. San Diego: Lucent Books, 1989. An overview of the Black Death for young readers.

Daniel Cohen, *The Black Death*. New York: Franklin Watts, 1974. Overview of the Black Death for young readers, nicely illustrated with images from medieval art.

Daniel Defoe, *A Journal of the Plague Year*. New York: Signet Classics, 1960. Fictionalized but historically accurate account of the great plague of London in 1665 by the author of *Robinson Crusoe*.

The Editors of Time-Life Books, *The Age of Calamity Time Frame AD 1300–1400*. Alexandria, VA: Time-Life Books, 1989. Beautifully illustrated overview of the fourteenth century; includes a brief pictorial treatment of the Black Death.

Jean Gimpel, *The Cathedral Builders*. Trans. Carl F. Barnes Jr. New York: Grove Press, 1961. Focuses on the great burst of cathedral building that took place during the Middle Ages.

Walter Olesky, *The Black Plague*. New York: Franklin Watts, 1982. Traces the history of the plague from ancient times to today, focusing on the Black Death and its aftermath in the Middle Ages. Also discusses causes and cures of the disease. For young readers.

John Ricker and John Saywell, *The Emergence of Europe*. Evanston, IL: McDougal, Littell, 1976. An overview of the development of European civilization from prehistory to the eve of the Renaissance. For young adults. Many good illustrations.

Derek Turner, *The Black Death*. Essex, UK: Longman, 1978. Good overview of the Black Death in England. Targeted at young British readers.

Works Consulted

Giovanni Boccaccio, *The Decameron*. Trans. G. H. McWilliam. New York: Penguin Books, 1983. A classic of world literature, these tales are told over ten days by ten young Florentine patricians seeking refuge in the country from the Black Death. Boccaccio's introduction to the tales contains the most vivid and often quoted description of the plague in Florence.

Norman F. Cantor, *The Civilization of the Middle Ages*. New York: HarperCollins, 1993. A comprehensive general history focusing on the culture and religion of the Middle Ages.

Norman Cohn, *The Pursuit of the Millennium*. New York: Oxford University Press, 1970. A study of revolutionary millenarians and mystical anarchists; includes a chapter on the flagellant movement.

G. G. Coulton, *Medieval Panorama*. Cambridge, England: Cambridge University Press, 1939. Scholarly overview of various aspects of medieval life; includes a chapter on the Black Death.

Georges Duby, *The Three Orders: Feudal Society Imagined*. Trans. Arthur Goldhammer. Chicago: University of Chicago Press, 1980. Scholarly study of the three social orders in medieval society.

Wallace K. Ferguson, *Europe in Transition 1300–1520*. Boston: Houghton Mifflin, 1962. Detailed discussion of the period of transition from feudal society to modern civilization.

Jean Froissart, *Chronicles of England, France, and Spain*. Trans. Thomas Johnes. New York: E. P. Dutton, 1911. This fourteenth-century French historian offers a contemporary account of important events of that century.

Robert Gottfried, *The Black Death*. New York: The Free Press, 1983. Complete account of the plague pandemic, with a focus on the ecological factors influencing the epidemics.

Denys Hay, *Europe in the Fourteenth and Fifteenth Centuries*. London: Longman, 1966. Overview of the fourteenth and fifteenth centuries with a brief discussion of conditions prior to the Black Death and some of its effects.

John Keegan, *A History of Warfare*. New York: Vintage Books, 1993. An interesting and learned study of warfare by a distinguished military historian; includes account of the Mongol warriors.

William Langland, *Piers the Ploughman*. Trans. J. F. Goodridge. New York: Penguin Books, 1959. A readable prose translation of the classic poem written shortly after the end of the Black Death.

William H. McNeill, *Plagues and Peoples*. Garden City, NY: Anchor Press/Doubleday, 1976. A study of the impact that infectious diseases have had on human society and civilizations from prehistoric times to the present.

Michael Pradwin, *The Mongol Empire: Its Rise and Legacy*. Trans. Eden and Cedar Paul. New York: The Free Press, 1967. Detailed study of the rise and fall of the Mongol empire.

Henry Sigerist, *Civilization and Disease.* Ithaca, NY: Cornell University Press, 1943. A scholarly study of how civilization has viewed disease through the ages.

R. W. Southern, *The Making of the Middle Ages.* New Haven, CT: Yale University Press, 1953. An overview of the major elements of medieval society.

Barbara Tuchman, *A Distant Mirror: The Calamitous 14th Century.* New York: Alfred A. Knopf, 1978. Thorough, readable history of the fourteenth century, focusing on one French family; includes a chapter on the Black Death.

Jean de Venette, *The Chronicle of Jean de Venette.* Trans. Jean Birdsall. New York: Columbia University Press, 1953. The chronicles of a French Carmelite friar, covering the years 1340 through 1368.

Philip Ziegler, *The Black Death.* New York: John Day Company, 1969. Thorough study of the Black Death, with strong focus on England.

Additional Works Consulted

Robert Forster and Orest Ranum, eds., *Biology of Man in History: Selections from the Annales Economies, Societes, Civilisations.* Trans. Elborg Forster and Patrician Ranum. Baltimore: Johns Hopkins University Press, 1975. A collection of essays on aspects of human biology in various periods of history. Contains an essay on Justinian's plague in the Early Middle Ages.

F. J. C. Hearnshaw, ed., *Medieval Contributions to Modern Civilization.* 1921. Reprint, Port Washington, NY: Kennikat Press, 1966. A collection of lectures by eminent British historians covering various aspects of medieval society. Very dry.

R. H. Hilton, ed., *Peasants, Knights, and Heretics.* New York: Cambridge University Press, 1976. A collection of scholarly articles discussing aspects of medieval social history. Contains article on the famine and agricultural crisis of 1317–1322.

Jacques LeGoff, *Time, Work, & Culture in the Middle Ages.* Trans. Arthur Goldhammer. Chicago: University of Chicago Press, 1980. Scholarly study of the these three elements of medieval life. Good discussion of ecclesiastical versus secular view of time in the Middle Ages.

David Nicholas, *The Domestic Life of a Medieval City: Women, Children, and the Family in Fourteenth-Century Ghent.* Lincoln: University of Nebraska Press, 1985. Detailed and scholarly reconstruction of the lives of women and children in the northern European city of Ghent during the fourteenth century.

Herman Styler, *The Plague Fighters.* Philadelphia: Chilton Company, 1960. A look at some of the plagues that have been a factor in human history.

Index

De Venette, Jean, 42, 77
Di Tura, Agnolo, 39
doctors
    advice on avoiding
        plague, 60–61
    code of ethics for, 96
    decline in numbers of, 95
    reaction to plague, 49, 50
    surgeons as, 95
    treated the plague, 63–64

education, 91–93
Egypt, 30–31
England
    Black Death reaches, 44
    manors in, 46–47
    mortality estimates, 50
    official language of, 92
    Peasants' Revolt in, 84–86
    war with France, 26
English, 92
environmental theories,
    58–59
epidemics, 11
Europe
    after the Black Death
        economic changes in,
            81, 90–91
        education in, 91–93
        landscape changes in,
            89–90
    prior to the Black Death
        church's role in, 18–19
        climate changes in,
            23–24
        famine in, 24–25
        feudalism in, 14
        manorial system in,
            15–18
        map of, 13
        peace, 13–14, 23
        population of, 14
        rural life in, 20

social classes in, 19
town and city life in,
    20–23
see also specific countries

families, 34, 54–55
famines, 18, 24, 25
farming
    prior to the Black Death,
        14, 16, 17
    shifts to eastern Europe,
        89–90
feudalism, 14, 19
Finland, 42
flagellant movement, 66–70
    in Germany, 68
    origins of, 67
    responses to, 69–70
fleas, 27, 32
Florence (Italy)
    currency in, 84
    the plague in, 33, 35–36
    trade in, 36
food shortages, 18, 24, 25
forests, 23, 89, 90
France
    Black Death reaches, 41
    mortality estimates,
        42–43, 49, 53
    peasant's revolt in, 82–83
    plague in rural, 42–44
    war with England, 26
funerals, 34–35, 36

Genoa (Italy), 37–38
Germany, 21, 42, 68, 73
Gobi Desert, 27, 28
government, 51
Greeks, 93
Greenland, 46
guilds, 22, 51

Hay, Denys, 23
head tax, 85

hedonism, 75–76
heriot, 16
High Middle Ages
    peace during, 13–14
    Roman Church's role,
        18–19
Holland, 42
homicide, 74
hospitals, 49, 95–96
Hotel-Dieu (hospital), 49
humanism movement, 93
humors (in body), 59–60
Hundred Years' War,
    25–26, 82–83

Iberia, 71
individualism, 75, 97
Ireland, 42
Islam, 30–31
Italy
    banking and trade in,
        22–23
    Black Death reaches,
        31–32
    famine-stricken riots in,
        25
    mortality estimates, 33,
        36, 38, 40
    workers revolt in, 84

Jacquerie, the, 82–83
Jews, 70–73
Justinian's plague, 11

Khaldun, Ibn, 30
King Edward III (of
    England), 43, 50
King Richard II (of
    England), 85–86
knights, 14

labor
    cost of, 80–81

Picture Credits

Cover photo: The Bettmann Archive

Archive Photos, 21, 95

The Bettmann Archive, 10, 11, 15, 32, 35, 59 (both), 64, 80

Bibliotheque Nationale, 26, 83

Corbis-Bettmann, 48, 67

Hulton Deutsch Collection Limited, 24 (top), 45, 53, 71, 73

Library of Congress, 38, 40, 46, 60, 63, 65, 68, 77, 84, 86, 94

The Mansell Collection, 37

National Institute of Health, 87

National Library of Medicine, 34, 39, 54, 78, 88, 97

North Wind Picture Archives, 14 (both), 16 (both), 19, 24 (bottom), 27, 30, 47, 50, 66, 74, 89, 91, 96

Picture Book of Devils, Demons and Witchcraft by Ernst and Johanna Lehner; published by Dover Publications, Inc., 43, 56

Stock Montage, Inc., 31, 70, 81, 92

About the Author

Phyllis Corzine received a B.A. in literature and language from Webster University in St. Louis and an M.A. in English and American literature from Washington University, St. Louis. She worked as an editor of educational materials for elementary and high school students for five years.

For the past five years, she has taught English and worked as a freelance writer. This is her second book for Lucent Books. Her first, published in 1995, is *The French Revolution*. Her other work includes a variety of educational materials as well as an adventure novel for young adults.

Corzine lives in St. Louis and has three children and three grandchildren. In her spare time she enjoys reading and gardening.